ALWAYS SICK, ALWAYS LOVED

Hope for Families Living
with a Chronic Illness

By
MICHAEL AND MARGARET ROBBLE

Copyright © 2015 by Michael and Margaret Robble

Always Sick, Always Loved
Hope for Families Living with a Chronic Illness
by Michael and Margaret Robble

Printed in the United States of America.

ISBN 9781498426992

All rights reserved solely by the author. The author guarantees all contents are original and do not infringe upon the legal rights of any other person or work. No part of this book may be reproduced in any form without the permission of the author. The views expressed in this book are not necessarily those of the publisher.

Unless otherwise indicated, scripture quotations taken from the English Standard Version (ESV). Copyright © 2001 by Crossway, a publishing ministry of Good News Publishers. Used by permission. All rights reserved.

www.xulonpress.com

This book is dedicated to everyone who suffers from a chronic health condition, and to those who sacrificially care for them. "Our hope for you is unshaken, for we know that as you share in our sufferings, you will also share in our comfort."
(2 Corinthians 1:7)

Table of Contents

Forward. vii
Preface ix
Introduction xiii

Chapter 1: "The Bitter Pill of Chronic Illness" 19
Chapter 2: "The Gospel and Chronic Disease" 44
Chapter 3: "A Healthy Doctrine of Suffering". 84
Chapter 4: "God Understands Your World" 103
Chapter 5: "Learning Contentment". 126
Chapter 6: "Practical Encouragements" 154
        (with Margaret's Reflections)
Chapter 7: "Eternal Hope". 221

Endnotes. 263

Forward

This is a unique book. It tells the story of a family facing the challenges of chronic illness in a way that takes you into the very real-life situations that are unknown to anyone unless they too have been there. But it is a story that is also packed with the hope found in the very real presence and power of God as demonstrated in the life of Michael and Margaret Robble. Follow them through the surprises and difficulties of life and of the challenges to faith and you will find on these pages the truth of how the message of the gospel (who God is and what he has done for us as revealed in Christ Jesus), gives hope and strength and power for living, regardless of the circumstances faced.

If you suffer from an ongoing illness, this book will serve you. If your family deals with the challenges of a chronically ill member, or you are the primary caregiver, this book will encourage you. If you want to get a window into the life of one such family and see how God meets them, please read this book. And for any pastor who wants to understand the world of such a family so that he may better understand and care for those in similar situations, this book is a gift and it will serve you.

Glynn McKenzie, Senior Pastor, Grace Community Church, Westminster, Colorado
June 2014

Preface

"Grace to you and peace from God our Father and the Lord Jesus Christ. Blessed be the God and Father of our Lord Jesus Christ, the Father of mercies and God of all comfort, who comforts us in all our affliction, so that we may be able to comfort those who are in any affliction, with the comfort with which we ourselves are comforted by God" (2 Corinthians 1:2-3).

Comfort in our suffering: it is what we all long for. When life's troubles hit us hard, in the depths of our souls we want to know that somehow we will successfully survive. We want to be assured, despite the confusion that hardship brings, that we are still loved and cared for. Particularly when a chronic health condition invades our lives, with its barbs of longevity, disability, and pain, we long to know for certain that we will have the strength to endure. We thirst for the assurance that no matter how medically bad things become, we will not be forsaken and left to fend for ourselves. We desire a real hope and consolation that helps us

Always Sick, Always Loved

understand that all our pain does have a purpose, even if that purpose is beyond our ability to understand.

Does this type of comfort exist? Is it possible, even when facing the prognosis of years of chronic disease and disability, to have love, peace, and hope in our hearts? Is there really a way to experience supernatural strength to persevere through years of illness, whether as a patient or caregiver? Well, this is what our book is all about—the help that can only come from the "God of all comfort."

Maybe you have just received some very troubling medical news, and wonder how you will be able to endure such a heart-wrenching prognosis. Maybe you are a patient who for years has had to live with the prison-like reality of limitations caused by a serious illness or disability. Maybe you are a caregiver, who, through the daily grind of sacrificial care for a loved one, finds yourself exhausted and disillusioned.

Have you ever wondered, "Where is God in all this medical turmoil? Why have I been dealt this hand of trouble? Is the Lord angry at me, and therefore punishing me for something I have done or haven't done?" We have asked ourselves these questions and a host of others over the years. Let's face it—suffering is difficult and confusing. Yet to find comfort in our medical chaos we must also seek answers to questions like these: "Does God make provision for the chronic sufferer? Is there real love, hope, peace, and help for the sick and disabled?"

Always Sick, Always Loved hits head-on the issues a family faces when confronted with a serious medical condition—Yes, you will see firsthand what the Robble family has been up against these past several years. But

Preface

most importantly, you will read about how we have experienced the inner strength necessary to endure.

You see, this book has been forged through our journey of almost twenty-five years living with an incurable and disabling autoimmune disease. This disease has completely changed the course of our lives, and continues to bring us a steady assault of medical challenges. Yet we have hope—not a hope in a fairly-tale-like happy ending to our illness journey, but a hope that far exceeds the limits of human effort or determination. This hope is a hope that only God can provide.

Our prayer is that first and foremost families suffering with a chronic disease or disability will be encouraged by our book. Whether you are a patient or caregiver, may the Lord help you to understand that you are not alone in your struggles. May he help you to see his love for you and your family, and to understand he truly is the One to go to for strength in your time of need.

Secondly, if you are not currently facing serious medical challenges, we pray our book will help you to better understand what the chronically ill and their families are going through. May God give you added insight to help you care for and comfort those who are sick or disabled, and we pray that this added insight will also help prepare you for what medically lies ahead.

Thirdly, if you are a pastor, our prayer is that *Always Sick, Always Loved* will enrich your ability to minister to those in your congregation who are physically suffering. May the Lord use our book as a resource to help you bring the compassion and the love of Jesus to patients and their caregivers.

As a final note, this book could never have been written without the prayers, encouragement, feedback, and example of others we have known and loved. So our deep gratitude goes out first to our parents, John and Dorothy Robble and Pete and Grace Aldrich, for their example of honoring their marriage covenant for over fifty years. It also goes to our pastors, Glynn McKenzie (senior pastor of Grace Community Church in Westminster, Colorado) and Trey Richardson (assistant pastor of Sovereign Grace Church in Gilbert, Arizona)—thank you as well for all your editing insights, support, love and care. To our dear friends here in Colorado who read the manuscript and consistently encouraged us—Eddie and GayAnn Dalton, Stan and Debby Tweten, Pete and Cindi Smith, Daniel and Jamie Frampton, and Anne Marie Hochhalter—we can't thank you enough. Lastly, to Robert and Barbara Beers, thank you for over thirty years of friendship, and for cheering us on to complete this book.

Michael Robble, July 2014

Introduction

I remember well that bright Saturday afternoon a number of years ago. As I sat on our living room couch in search of some relaxing sports programming, my then seven-year-old son quietly walked into the room. Caleb's deep brown eyes and expressive face immediately captured my attention. "Dad," he asked sheepishly, "could you pitch me a few in the backyard?" His boyish sincerity instantly vetoed my television plans.

I pulled myself off the couch and stepped out our back door into the brilliant Colorado sunshine. Caleb already had his black plastic bat in hand, and was taking numerous left-handed practice swings as I located the large sponge-like softball I was to pitch to him. Since the flight of a batted ball is quite unpredictable, this super-soft softball was the safest means to an enjoyable time of backyard baseball.

As I readied myself to bring some low-arching, low-velocity underhand tosses, Caleb dug in his feet. Seeing my son's eagerness put a smile on my face. I knew my primary mission was to give him the opportunity to hit the ball as hard as he wanted to. My first slow toss was clobbered deep into the chain link fence on the north side of our yard. My second was rocketed a few feet over my head and didn't stop rolling until it hit the east side fence. Soon another pitch was crushed high and long over the roof of our house. My pitching mission was being accomplished, but I wondered if a bit more intense "stuff" could bring a new depth of challenge to my little man.

I felt a sudden moment of inspiration. I recalled the story of pitcher Jimmy Morris, depicted so well in Disney's movie *The Rookie*. Morris was old (well, almost forty) and discovered he could throw a baseball at a speed of almost one hundred miles per hour. Why couldn't I, a man in my mid-forties, bring a little heat to my seven-year-old?

I gave my son an intense, competitive stare. As I leaned toward him with the ball in my pitching hand, I said to him, "Caleb, do you want me to bring you some heat?" He confidently nodded in anticipation. Instantly my imagination kicked in. I was no longer the middle-aged dad in his Colorado backyard. Now I was the fire-balling right-hander originally from upstate New York. I looked in for the sign. I grunted. I twirled the ball in my pitching hand. I rocked, kicked, and delivered. Caleb swung and missed. I looked in for the imaginary sign again. Another overhand fastball. Another swing and a miss. There would be no more towering shots over the roof today. The only thing that oversized softball hit for the next ten minutes was the chain link fence behind Caleb. I must confess, it felt good to show him a little old fashioned hardball.

Do you think I was cruel blowing pitches past my son? Well, my payback came just minutes later. I

Introduction

walked slowly back into the house, dripping sweat, and feeling a few muscles I didn't know I had. My right arm felt heavy and tired. My legs ached as if I'd run a few miles. On the emotional front, it dawned on me that repeatedly striking out my son wasn't anything to glory in, though he did seem to enjoy the challenge of trying to hit a daddy fastball.

A few days later the pain in my right elbow began. First it was a dull annoyance, but within a short period of time it grew into a throbbing hindrance. Despite my determination to avoid seeing my doctor, I finally humbled myself and went to see him. After a short examination, he determined I had tendonitis of the elbow, caused by less than thirty of my pseudo-fast-balls. He also went out of his way to tell me that he "normally" saw this kind of condition in athletes. Based on my not-so-toned physique, clearly I was the exception. Ibuprofen, ice, and stretching exercises were prescribed for the next four weeks. After this regimen my arm was finally back to normal. Was I getting old or what?

As hard as it might have been for me to accept, my arm pain was just a small glimpse of what I am physically headed for. Like it or not, my body is slowly wearing out. Unlike popular car models, I don't come with some special multi-year drive train warranty. The reality is that my body is frail. Thirty overhand heaters sent me to a doctor's office. Don't get me wrong—I try to take care of myself. Yet I, like everyone else, finds my body is aging. It is prone to injury and disease. The more years I live, the less I am physically able to do.

Today literally millions of Americans are reminded daily of their mortality. Some, after years of activity, find themselves hindered in their twilight years by a crippling chronic disease. Others have never known a life of physical activity. Afflicted in their youth, these folks continue to try to live their lives knowing they will never be able to do the things most people take for granted. Most heart-wrenching of all are the sick and disabled children, struggling to grow up under the weight of chronic health problems. Yes, disabling health conditions can permeate any season of a person's life.

Also, not-to-be overlooked, in every medical scenario there is a second patient. Patient number two may not be taking medications or frequently enduring an array of medical tests, but he or she is nonetheless greatly impacted by chronic disease. The second patient is the primary caregiver. Handed the responsibility of daily (if not moment by moment) tending to the needs of the patient, medical duties permeate his or her life. She may be the mom who spends virtually every waking moment making sure her child with Down syndrome is secure and lovingly cared for. He may be the son who has brought his aging mother into his home, and spends countless hours each month tending to her needs. She may be the wife whose treasured husband is stricken with the disabling effects of Parkinson's disease, and she is determined to see to it that he gets all the care he needs. Yes, every medical drama has its second patient, the caregiver—the person experiencing the significant responsibilities that come with giving care to the chronically ill.

Even if you are not currently a patient or a caregiver, I'd like to encourage you to let the truths communicated in our book help prepare you for that season

Introduction

in your life. With medical advances and increased life expectancy, most of us will one day be faced with a disabling health condition or the life-changing decision to provide care for a chronically ill family member.

It is our prayer, then, that patients, caregivers, and those who may one day be a patient or caregiver will be encouraged through the reading of this book. It is written with the prayer that you may find fresh hope and strength in the midst of your current medical circumstances, and wisdom to help prepare yourself for the medical trials that will be coming your way.

Some of the questions we will attempt to face in *Always Sick, Always Loved* are the difficult and troubling ones: Why has God allowed this physical affliction in my family? Does he really understand what we are going through? Is there power in the gospel of Jesus Christ to help us endure even if the illness stays for years? What biblical truths are there to hold on to that can give me hope even if my medical circumstances persist or get worse? How can I be a caregiver who honors the Lord in my efforts to help a sick loved one?

This book is also your invitation to come into our lives, and see what the Savior has done for us. You will notice we have decided to be very transparent in our writing. Prepare yourself to hear about our struggles, both externally and internally, which means you will read about the sad news of our discouragement, bitterness, and other sins. But more importantly, get ready to hear about the amazing forgiveness and redemption we have in Christ, and how even through years of chronic disease God has given us hope, joy, love, and peace through the power of the cross.

Finally, I would like to conclude this introduction by honoring my precious wife Margaret, whom I have had the privilege of being married to these past twenty-five years. Despite the progression of her disease and her frequent severe physical pain, she continues to consistently demonstrate the joy of the Lord to me and our children, and cares for us in an amazing way. Margaret, I love you, and thank you for showing me how powerful God's grace is on a daily basis. Thank you as well for all your support and contributions to our book.

Chapter One
"The Bitter Pill of Chronic Illness"

> "For we do not want you to be ignorant, brothers, of the affliction we experienced in Asia. For we were so utterly burdened beyond our strength that we despaired of life itself. Indeed, we felt that we had received the sentence of death. But that was to make us rely not on ourselves, but on God who raises the dead" (2 Corinthians 1:8-9).

I begin this writing with some reality-based sad news. Our physical bodies are slowly breaking down. Our once-dependable strength is becoming a bit undependable. Our hair is thinning, our joints are weakening, and tasks we once took for granted are becoming more challenging. I remember a Saturday afternoon when I decided to do some yard work. After about an hour of trimming bushes and raking leftover fall leaves, I decided to give my red Geo Prizm a much needed car wash. As I soaped down the passenger side front door,

I suddenly felt a sharp stabbing pain in my lower back. The formula was simple: yard work + car washing = muscle pain.

Yes, my body is aging. I try to exercise, eat "right," and take care of myself. Yet I am physically slowing down. I have not been given an exemption from weakness and pain. It comes to all of us at one time or another. So the question is this: Are we prepared for the arrival of physical weakness? Do we accept the fact that our bodies will breakdown and eventually we or someone we love will develop a chronic health condition? I don't believe this is a fatalistic, pessimistic mindset. It is a mortal reality.

D.A. Carson said it well. "The truth of the matter is that all we have to do is live long enough, and we will suffer. Our loved ones will die, we ourselves will be afflicted with some disease or other."[1] I would summarize and supplement Dr. Carson's words by saying, "All we have to do is live long enough and we or someone we love will have a chronic health condition." This is not just my personal opinion. The medical statistics speak for themselves. "90% of seniors have at least one chronic disease and 77% have two or more chronic diseases."[2]

Yet chronic disease is not just the challenge of the elderly and their families. Literally millions of Americans suffer chronic health conditions well before they are eligible for their AARP® card. Saddest of all are childhood illnesses and disabilities, which break the hearts of parents, as they see their precious child suffer the pain and disruption of health problems.

When Margaret and I met, little did we know that a chronic disease was soon to follow. Yet for reasons beyond our ability to understand, the disease came, and it came with a seemingly merciless vengeance. I think it is imperative at this point to hear from Margaret directly. Her recollection of the events of a little over twenty-five years ago make it clear how swiftly and all consuming the arrival of a chronic illness can be.

The Surprise Invasion

Okay, Michael's been encouraging me to write this "Chapter One" story, so I'll see what I can do. He's titled it "The Surprise Invasion" which to me could conjure up all sorts of situations. So, I'm not sure if *I'm* the surprise invasion, or if *he* is the surprise invasion. Read on, and you'll see who or what "The Surprise Invasion" really is. I think I'll start with how I met this man that God has so wonderfully and generously given me.

At the age of thirty-four, I was still single, waiting somewhat patiently for a husband. My list of what I desired in a husband amazingly dwindled from 134 requirements that he must meet to *one*—and that one was that he must love the Lord more than I do. Then I began to think maybe "he" just wasn't part of God's plan for my life.

In the summer of 1988, I took a trip to Israel with my good friend Annie, along with a church group. After years of being a nurse's assistant and not doing much but baby-sitting and working, this trip stirred my heart to new heights of adventure. I felt like this was my new life. I was finally laying down my desire for a husband and family. After returning I intended to finish nursing school, move to Israel and live on a kibbutz. It sounded like a plan to me, and it was very exciting. I think the

Always Sick, Always Loved

people I talked to in Israel thought I was nuts, but to humor me, they said they would only let me back in the country if I could contribute something to their country.

So, Annie and I returned to New York charged and ready to go. Annie got into nursing school, while I was trying to figure out how to pay for it. Every verse I read seemed to confirm this was the direction I was being led in, and each morning the Lord seemed to be speaking oh-so clearly to me about Israel: this was my future! Often after church I would discuss my plans with one of our pastors, who was not as excited as we were. Two single women, heading out to a country that is something of a political and biblical hot seat. But to us this just made it more appealing. Never one to be really brave, I figured my desire to go to a country where bombings, shootings and terrorists were a part of existence must be a *definite* sign from God!

Then one Sunday, while I was discussing my plans with the pastor, a young man I didn't really know butted into our conversation, adding things like "I don't think this is a good idea" or "You could get shot." Well, I *knew* that—that was the exciting part! Besides, who is this guy? And what did he know about *my* life? I was furious that some stranger would have the audacity to question God's plan for my life. This was *me and God*, not *you* buddy—whoever you are! But he didn't go away. In fact, he started asking me to go for walks with him. Now how could I work, try to get into school, make my big plans and go for a walk with him every night! But I went—In fact, I started getting in good shape after a while because we walked all over town. Here I had been praying for a husband so long and thought I had

"The Bitter Pill of Chronic Illness"

finally laid it down. I was angry that this guy had the nerve to mess things up. Annie got to the point that she came to me, looking quite disturbed, telling me she figured I wasn't going to keep with "the plan."

About a month after we first met, my new "walking partner" suggested perhaps we should pray about getting married. I was stunned—a month? We hadn't even had a fight yet. But you get what you pray for. We fought. Three months after that, he officially, with my dad's blessing, asked me to be his wife on Valentine's Day of 1989. Actually my dad, who is almost totally deaf, misunderstood him. He thought Michael was asking for permission for us to elope. He still said yes. Thanks, Dad.

About a month after this wonderful event, I began having searing chest pains, difficulty breathing, and joint pain—along with various other symptoms that didn't go along with planning our August 19th wedding. I worked less and less, went to more and more doctors, and received diagnoses that ran from asthma to "it's all in your head."

My prayer for a husband who was godlier than I proved to be the greatest blessing of my life. Michael never complained, never stopped crying out to God for answers, never stopped seeking the Lord for what this meant for our lives. He never once told me that he didn't want to marry a woman who was suddenly unable to do most of the things I had been able to do just weeks before. He patiently and lovingly planned our wedding. I think the only thing I did without him was to pick out my wedding dress.

Our wedding was beautiful and it was the most joyful day of my life. God had heard my cry throughout

Always Sick, Always Loved

so many years for a godly husband and that husband was standing next to me. But after the wedding was the honeymoon. Oh my—I was so sick, but trying to feel so healthy. Still striving under the word that this was all in my head, I felt like such a terrible wife for this wonderful man who deserved so much better than what I could give him.

The most painful thing we were learning during this time was that if people don't understand your illness, you end up going through the trial very alone. Most of our friends also tended to believe that what I was experiencing was all in my head. They thought for some reason I was trying to draw attention to myself by being sick. I cried out to God, asking him that if this were true, to please forgive me and help me to see how to change. God's timing in bringing Michael into my life was amazing, since he soon became not only my best friend but also, it appeared, my only friend.

The first year of our marriage was solidified by our desire to hear God, obey him, and find out what was wrong with me. But we were also becoming more and more isolated by something that neither we, nor any of our friends, could understand.

The day we returned from our honeymoon, Michael saw my doctor who told him that it appeared I had lupus, a mysterious immune system disease, which we had never heard of. The doctor said that apart from a miracle, I would have it for the rest of my life. Many of those closest to us still questioned whether this was still just something in my head, so Michael decided for two months to not tell me what the doctor had told him. We have discussed this many times, and clearly this was not a wise choice of action. A husband and

"The Bitter Pill of Chronic Illness"

wife need to both understand an illness *together*—not just one carrying the burden alone.

Our first year together became one of loneliness and survival. I remember so many times that Michael would come home from work and I would be lying on the bed, propped up and trying to breathe, asking God to let me die. Michael would be next to me, crying out to God to not listen to me! Every breath felt like knives going through my ribs, so not breathing seemed like the most logical solution. Avoiding deeply breathing resulted in many fainting episodes—many times from hyperventilating, sometimes just from the pain of taking a breath. Simple tasks like taking a dish from the cupboard became impossible, along with doing laundry, driving, and grocery shopping. Slowly all the normal every day responsibilities of a wife became more difficult for me to do. Those difficult days became a blur of pain and loneliness, but there was always the joy of having Michael to walk through that with me.

After a year and a half, my doctor recommended that we move to a drier climate. The weather of upstate New York, particularly its high humidity and cold, damp winters, were making my symptoms worse. My physician had just been to a medical conference in Phoenix, and seeing how dry it was, she suggested it was worth a try for us to check out the climate. It was either that or take high doses of prednisone. If we opted for the prednisone, she felt that I might die within a fifteen year period, meaning the steroids would kill me before the lupus would.

My parents, who were also living in upstate New York, were about to take a vacation to Arizona and offered to rent an apartment that would be big enough

Always Sick, Always Loved

for all of us. Michael got a leave of absence from his teaching job and we were off to the desert. Amazingly, within twenty-four hours of being in the desert climate, I was swimming laps in the pool, taking walks with Michael, shopping, cooking—most of the things that had become a distant memory were now back. There was still some pain and definitely fatigue, but it was obvious that things looked better in the Southwest. We enjoyed that month, but with the joy came the realization that God may be moving us across the country, away from our families and everyone we had ever known.

When we returned from our month of sunshine and renewed health, it took only twenty-four hours for all my symptoms to come back as furious as before. Again I found myself almost completely incapacitated. Michael prayed earnestly to hear God's leading. Within a few weeks he began his search for a teaching job in southern Arizona, anywhere that seemed like desert, convinced that it was the Lord's will for us to relocate. Within a few months, God provided a job in the northern part of Phoenix.

In late June of 1991, we were packed and leaving upstate New York, the place we had lived all our lives. It was a good thing that I was as weak as I was, rendered helpless as Michael moved us away from our families, crying through each state as we went. I kept thinking how much Michael began to look like Abraham. God said *"Go!"* and we went.

So, "The Surprise Invasion" turned out to be a sickness that invaded my body and has no cure. Not in my wildest dreams would I have imagined that this would be the path we would be on. As you will see, it has affected virtually every year of our marriage. It seems to have come to stay.

The Long Occupation

Margaret's illness came upon us suddenly. Its arrival wasn't a prelude to a short stretch of sickness. It was the introduction to decades of medical challenges. Her body no longer moved without pain. Even breathing could instigate crushing, burning chest pain. Our lives were thrown into the sea of physical distress with all its waves of complication. No longer were we the happy married couple savoring the honeymoon years. In our first year as husband and wife we were thrust into the roles of patient and caregiver. We poured our hearts out to God, earnestly trying to unravel the confusion of why he would allow such a thing to happen to us.

Webster's New World Dictionary defines "chronic" as "lasting a long time or recurring. . . having an ailment for a long time. . . habitual."[3] A *long time. . . habitual.* These words don't naturally inspire someone to hope. The affliction is here to stay. It will probably be a part of your life for the rest of your life.

Just weeks after we were married we got the chronic medical forecast. Her doctor bluntly put it this way: "Autoimmune diseases like this are incurable. We can treat the symptoms, but we cannot cure the disease. Adjust your life for the best quality of life with the disease, for the disease will *always* be there."

In the summer of 1991, Margaret's illness propelled us out of upstate New York and into the Arizona desert. Having lived in the small, rural town of Cortland, NY—which had about seven traffic lights and closed Main Street each summer for the annual Dairy Parade—moving to Metro Phoenix was like relocating to another planet. The Valley of the Sun had traffic, millions of people, and streets so equally spaced that it reminded me of a piece of graph paper. No more scenic drives through the green, well-watered countryside. Dry, desert air and searing heat were God's treatment to give us a better quality of life.

In our first seven years on "planet Phoenix," Margaret was able to enjoy seasons of remission, could drive and grocery shop, and even worked a few part-time jobs. Though I wouldn't describe our life as normal (since weather changes still gave her searing joint and chest pain), the disease was manageable. 1992 to 1997 were probably her best years physically, and, though it was difficult being so far away from our families, we felt God had blessed us with a place where we could have a fairly normal life.

During these years we were able to experience many special blessings. On the employment side, I was able to establish myself as a "mathematical fixture" at Dobson High School in Mesa. Being a part of the math department there gave me valuable experience and secure employment. Despite the fact that I kept going green with my math humor (i.e. recycling my jokes year after year) I was granted tenure in the district. Job security gave us stability and the sense that we were destined to live in Arizona for the long haul.

On the church side of things, Margaret and I had the joy of helping with children's ministry and youth ministry. Serving together in the church had always been our desire, and the searing desert climate gave her enough relief for us to serve others. Directing children's

"The Bitter Pill of Chronic Illness"

plays, organizing a vacation Bible school, and going on youth retreats were some of our most fulfilling experiences. It was great to be able to look beyond our medical challenges and bless other families.

Speaking of families—the Lord gave us the desire to pray about having children of our own. Since the first year of our marriage we had been trying to conceive. Yet always pressing on the back of my mind (particularly when we lived in New York) was how Margaret could physically endure a pregnancy. With her frequent chest and joint pain, picturing her as an expectant mother made pregnancy seem all too dangerous.

The improvement she was having in Phoenix made motherhood a much more realistic possibility, yet we were still not able to conceive. In the summer of 1994 her gynecologist discovered a large cyst on one of her ovaries, and informed us surgery would be required to remove it. After the operation, he first told Margaret that he was not able to get a picture of the cyst to show her, since it broke up upon removal. (She *really* likes to see these kinds of things, which is one of the great ways we complement each other—seeing photos like that tend to make me queasy). On the more serious side, he solemnly told us that with all the scar tissue he saw, we would probably never be able to conceive a child.

Though this news was emotionally crushing, within the next three years we were given our two richest Arizona blessings via adoption: our daughter Liz (born in August of 1995) and our son Caleb (born in March of 1997). Though I could easily write numerous pages describing the adventures we experienced to get them, I think the best way to summarize these two precious gifts is to quote Margaret's dad, Pete Aldrich. Upon seeing each of them for the first time, he gave a wry chuckle and exclaimed, "Yep, they are more beautiful than anything the two of you could have made."

We knew during these years in Phoenix that Margaret had an incurable disease, but it was more of an irritating nuisance, not an all-consuming hourly trial. Despite this nuisance factor, we were able to live a more normal, semi-active life. Margaret was living the joys (and challenges) of being a mom, caring for two children under the age of three. I was very busy with my high school teaching responsibilities, and we added to that mix our church activities. Yes, with the rain came the pain. Since the sun shined over three hundred days a year, the rain-pain combinations were quite spread out. It appeared we were now on the path of having a pretty typical life together, while acknowledging the reality that once in a while her autoimmune issues would give us some short-lived interruptions.

Diseases however, seldom seem content to lie dormant. We had no indication that Margaret's illness was readying itself to begin a more complete occupation. Over the next few years she began to have rain-like symptoms on some sunny days. It progressed to the point that she often awoke on cloudless mornings in so much pain that she needed my assistance to get out of bed. The burning pain in her joints and chest made any bodily movement an ordeal. Her doctors were baffled. Additionally, hot weather usually worsened the severity of her symptoms—not a welcome development in the Arizona sunshine.

By early 2000 her disease had reached consistent, chronic proportions. The low point of that year took

"The Bitter Pill of Chronic Illness"

place one night in August. Around 1:00 a.m. she awoke with such severe chest pain that she thought she was having a heart attack. I immediately called 911. I shall never forget the despair I felt as Margaret was wheeled to the ambulance. There she was, my precious wife, struggling to breathe under the cloak of an oxygen mask. "God, what is going on?" I thought. "Why are you allowing this to happen to us? What did we do to deserve this?"

As the next few days unfolded, it was determined Margaret had an inflammation around her heart. Her disease had decided that annoying joint and chest pain were not enough—it had to expand its spew of venom into her cardiovascular system. This harsh reality brought with it waves of fear and concern. Could her illness be her killer? How are we going to endure this? She was prescribed anti-inflammatory medications to treat her physical symptoms. I, on the other hand, was emotionally drained and spiritually perplexed. What was the Lord doing in our lives?

Crashing down upon me was a wave of questions with no concrete answers. Were my preschool-age children going to see their mother die? How could I continue to work and know she and the children were cared for? Why, after nearly a decade in Arizona, was her health getting worse in the heat? How could we possibly endure many more days (or years) of this intense trial? And on a deeper level, where was the love of God in all this? My spiritual track record was clear. The more I prayed, the more helpless I felt. I'd lie in bed asking God to heal her. She got worse. I invited the godliest people I knew to come over and pray for her. She got worse. I was totally baffled as to what to do next. I believed God was out there and the Bible said he was listening, but for some reason it appeared he had left us to suffer on our own.

Internally Margaret also began to have some serious spiritual struggles. She would often say to me, "Why is God punishing me? What did I do that is so awful that he would allow me so much pain? I must be a horrible Christian in God's eyes to keep getting beat up like this." Though I tried to encourage her, I felt I had little to say, for I felt as confused as (or more than) she did.

Despite my shaky faith, I tried daily to cry out to God. I knew our situation was too big for us, and I so wanted to hear from him. Over the next few months one thing became clear to me. We had to get out of the searing Arizona heat. To say that the prospect of moving again was overwhelming would be a considerable understatement. I figured we had already done the required move for her disease. We were settled into our church life. I was going full tilt in my teaching career, readying to finish my tenth year at Dobson High. Was it really possible, after all we'd already been through, that God was *really* telling me we had to move again?

Well, to be to the point, the answer was a clear "*Yes.*" After more weeks of prayer, counsel, and an extended scouting visit, Denver was to be our new home. It's a city with a dry, arid climate, and the coolness of the four seasons. Once again we were packing our things and saying goodbye to dear friends. In the summer of 2002 we relocated to metro Denver.

Our first couple of years in Colorado saw Margaret's health show some minor improvements. She was able

"The Bitter Pill of Chronic Illness"

to take occasional walks and bike rides in the much cooler climate. Her new doctors ran a bunch of fresh tests, some of which raised questions as to whether her diagnosis of lupus was really accurate. She clearly had some type of immune system disorder. The flare-ups of joint and chest pain confirmed that over and over again. Yet her primary care doctor didn't believe her symptoms accurately fit the lupus scenario. To our dismay, within a few years his suspicions were horribly verified.

As I mentioned before, chronic diseases seldom are content to lie dormant. At times their remission lulls us to believe they are gone for good. But, at an appointed time of opportunity, they spew their systemic venom again. For Margaret, the summer of 2005 brought the most horrendous invasion of her disease.

The clearest recollection I have of that time was the ever-increasing intensity of her symptoms. No longer did just the limiting effects of joint and chest pain torment her. In a very short period of time, burning pain in both ankles, mysterious high fevers, and a dose of mental confusion complicated her condition. The climax came one night around midnight. She awoke, burning with fever, looked directly into my eyes and said, "Who are you?" Though I suppose I have a forgettable face, Margaret's memory lapse gave me all the incentive I needed to get her to the hospital. Something was terribly wrong.

Three days into her hospital stay we were told a CT scan of her chest revealed enlarged lymph nodes. Her doctor said it was either lymphoma or sarcoidosis. A few weeks later a biopsy of her lymph nodes gave us conclusive results. The diagnosis was sarcoidosis.

Always Sick, Always Loved

"Sarcoid," as Margaret's doctors explained it, is an autoimmune disease that was first seen in the 1800's. Its symptoms are typically chronic pain and inflammation, lumps under the skin, and breathing problems. Often sarcoid can scar the lungs, leading to permanent lung damage. Left untreated, it can be fatal. Since it is difficult to diagnose, our doctor felt that it was most likely the disease she had had all along. Now we knew for sure (after thinking for sixteen years that it was lupus) what the real medical problem was. Could her sarcoidosis be treated and cured?

Though it was good news to finally know what her disease was, it was very sad news to hear her prognosis and treatment. Tormenting and discouraging medical words were thrown at us again. The disease is *incurable*. The sarcoid will probably be *chronic*. Maybe worst of all, the medication we will treat you with is *prednisone*. Prednisone—the steroid with all the horrible side effects. Expect weight gain, fluid retention, and a "moon face."

Her doctor told us that 85% of sarcoidosis patients experience a significant remission of the disease after a year of intense prednisone therapy. Given those stats, we decided to begin the steroid regimen in November of 2005. It started with 60mg a day, every day for a number of months. As predicted, within a short period of time Margaret's appearance began to change. Her face became more and more puffy. She gained weight. At times, she would weep in front of the mirror as she stared at her transformed appearance. Seeing her eyes become slits, wedged inside a steroid-inflated face, coupled with the bloating in the rest of her body was emotionally devastating to her. She wondered how I

"The Bitter Pill of Chronic Illness"

could possibly love her when she looked so awful. I tried my best to reassure her of my love, and often told her I loved her no matter what she looked like. Yet in her heart she feared that I would tire of caring for a sick wife, particularly one who looked so horrible. It seemed there was little I could say or do to console her.

To make matters even worse, during these prednisone months she developed pneumonia four different times. Colds would turn into bronchitis, then settle into her lungs as pneumonia. After a regimen of antibiotics and breathing treatments she would start to feel a bit better, only to see all the nasty symptoms return within a short period of time. The cyclic coughing up of colorful chunks and wheezing, combined with her altered appearance, was almost too much for her to bear. I had never seen Margaret so depressed. Some days she would tell me she just wanted to go home to be with Jesus. She felt like she just couldn't take anymore. Frankly I couldn't blame her. Being pain-free in heaven was a reasonable alternative to what she was going through.

Regretfully, during this time and the months that followed I had a sickness of my own. It was an illness of the soul. Though outwardly I tried to be strong for Margaret and our children, inwardly my heart was gradually becoming infected with a virus of apathy and hopelessness. I simply didn't feel we could take any more as a family. Her sarcoidosis-prednisone-pneumonia trilogy brought a measure of suffering that I *really* didn't understand. After all we had been through—the moves, the challenges, the sufferings—we were into our worst medical trial ever.

What did I do? I subtly and gradually grew indifferent toward God. My love and gratefulness to the Lord were displaced by a callousness and weariness. I was tired of the struggle. I was emotionally drained from seeing Margaret suffer day after day. I was weary of everything that came with a chronic disease. Instead of passionately turning to God, I quietly and selectively withdrew. I didn't outwardly rebel. I just started doubting in the goodness of God through it all. Hey, our lives were consumed with this disease, and I was only a man. I didn't get why it all had to keep continuing and getting even more severe. So, I spiritually pouted. Bitterness began to get a hold of me. I still read my Bible and prayed, but my hope was waning. I began to embrace an independent, survivor mentality.

Coupled with this, I lost hope in God's love coming through people. Our church family was where we could find encouragement, hope, and prayerful support. Yet during this time I didn't attend church functions regularly. To be sure, some days Margaret needed my care. Other days, however, I felt it just wasn't worth the effort to see people. I figured they wouldn't understand our situation, and probably would say trite things like "I know how you feel" or "I'll be praying for you" when they really didn't mean it. Sadly, losing hope in God affected my attitude toward others as well. I was actually distancing myself from those who cared about us the most.

Regretfully, I also became very apathetic regarding our money. Frankly, I had been careless with our finances for a number of years, but my increasing callousness and loss of hope made things worse. My pity-filled, survivor-mentality had led to financial

"The Bitter Pill of Chronic Illness"

indifference. Living on a budget and making wise decisions with our money were not of importance to me. Sure, over the past few years we had been handed some sizeable medical and moving costs that exceeded the capacity of my teacher's salary. Yet I didn't faithfully seek God's help. I neglected to arrange payment plans we could afford. I resisted humbling myself to get financial advice. I was consumed with just getting through the day.

My money strategy could be summarized this way: as increased medical costs came our way, I depended on my assortment of credit cards. My financial refuge was the cumulative "power" of the plastic I carried in my wallet. My hardness of heart and "I don't care about money" attitude steered me away from getting the counsel I desperately needed. We weren't making any extravagant purchases, so I just carelessly hoped for the best. So sadly the stage was set for our financial implosion.

By September of 2006 the fruit of my carelessness was clear. By consistently putting medical costs and other unplanned purchases on credit cards for a number of years, our overall debt had grown to over $75,000. Because we had such a high amount of debt, virtually all our creditors decided to raise our required minimum payments from 2% to 4% of our balances. Despite my pleas to them over the phone, no credit card company was willing to sympathize with our situation. Thus we were faced with over $1,300 per month in credit card payments.

Now each month I had to choose between credit card payments, her normal medical costs (which averaged over $400 per month), and our typical living expenses. For the first time in my life I fell behind in my payments. As we fell more and more behind, our creditors began to call our home with increased regularity. Sometimes creditors would call as many as ten to fifteen times a day. Inside our home we were daily dealing with the stress and challenge of Margaret's disease. Outside our home, collection agencies were now pounding us with the goal of getting at least a minimum payment.

The fusion of medical and financial trouble was a burden I felt we couldn't bear. I knew we had to find some means of financially settling with our creditors. On my teacher's salary and under ideal financial conditions, I was looking at over twenty years to pay off the debt. I finally humbled myself and met with my friend Don, a man of compassion whom I could trust. I handed him a typed list of every single debt and detail of our finances. Within a few minutes, he said to me, "Mike, have you ever considered bankruptcy?"

Bankruptcy—the scenario I thought I'd never face, particularly as a Christian. The prospect of bankruptcy filled my heart with fear, humiliation, and an overpowering sense of failure. Yet the more I prayed—(and after meeting with an attorney), the more I realized this was the best way for us to settle our debts. God knew the magnitude of our suffering, and he understood how much pressure we could handle. Even though I realized my apathy and carelessness had played a large role in getting us into this mess, here in the United States bankruptcy laws were created for a situation like ours. We couldn't fix Margaret's health, but we could resolve our financial woes. So in January of 2007 we filed for Chapter 7 bankruptcy. A month later, I wheeled

"The Bitter Pill of Chronic Illness"

Margaret, with her oxygen tank in tow, into Denver's bankruptcy court. In April of 2007 our case was finalized, bringing closure to our debt and giving us a fresh financial start in the midst of all our medical battles. Financially we had found a resolution—but the complexity of her health issues continued to grow.

By December of 2006 her doctors decided it was time to wean her off the prednisone. As the daily doses were reduced, though, Margaret found it increasingly difficult to walk. The steroids may have brought her lymph nodes back down to size, but they were also causing a load of side effects in the bones of her feet. Though I don't recall the medical term for it, her feet bones were breaking down, creating a bunch of microscopic fractures. The pain was severe and all-consuming. The medication prescribed to save her life was crippling her.

The difficulty she had in walking forced us to make some significant adjustments. We moved our bed from the upstairs master bedroom to the main level of our home. We had to rent a wheelchair. We purchased a portable toilet so she could go to the bathroom only a few feet from our bed. Because it was no longer safe for her to be home alone, we arranged for friends to stay with her while I was at work. Her ongoing deterioration was the saddest thing I had ever seen. My precious wife was losing her battle with sarcoidosis, and the medication designated to keep the disease in check had made her nearly an invalid. With no improvement three months after ending her prednisone treatment, I knew we had to take a more aggressive course of action.

In March of 2007 we decided to go to the Mayo Clinic in Scottsdale, Arizona. With some of the most brilliant medical minds in the country, the Mayo Clinic specializes in helping people with the most complex medical conditions. Our plan was to take two week-long trips—the first would be in April, the second in June. Almost five years after leaving Phoenix, we were heading back on a desperate medical journey.

From a personal standpoint, our return to Arizona was bittersweet. Coming back to the desert gave us the joy of reuniting with friends we hadn't seen in years, but every conversation was tainted by the uncertainty of Margaret's prognosis. Would God bring us favorable medical news in the Valley of the Sun? Or, as we feared, would we hear a medical forecast that would predict increased symptoms leading to her death?

To be brief, the doctors at Mayo confirmed her diagnosis of sarcoidosis. They told us her feet now showed no signs of micro-fractures (so it was time to put the bed back upstairs). Most of them felt the disease should not shorten her life (i.e. we should expect a normal life expectancy). The biggest question mark, however, was how much her sarcoidosis would continue to affect her on a daily basis. Some patients experience months (and possibly years) of sarcoid remission. Due to Margaret's age and the number of years she had probably had the disease, the doctors said remission for her would be a long shot. She would most likely wake up each day feeling the effects of sarcoid. Our goal would be to find the best treatment plan to give her the best quality of life with her illness.

After we arrived home from Mayo in June, Margaret began to carefully increase her activity level. Our bed returned upstairs (the kids and I had great fun sliding the mattress and box spring up the stairs) and we all rallied together to help her gain strength. It was a great relief to know she wasn't going to die from the disease. It continued to be difficult, however, to observe on a daily basis the crippling effects of sarcoidosis. The constant burning joint pain, the heart-attack-like chest pain (especially when weather fronts came through), and the steady burden of fatigue draped her body. She was alive, projected to live a long life, yet imprisoned by the inflammatory jail of this autoimmune disease. We continued to press on, learning to trust God along the way, and were grateful for medical gains like the parking of her wheelchair in our basement in August of 2007.

Now let's fast-forward to today (July 2014). In the past year, Margaret's condition has deteriorated significantly. The most life-threatening symptom has been her inability to consistently absorb protein, which has led to rapid weight loss and diminishing muscle strength. Though her weight has stabilized over the past few months, we are living in a very precarious time—so much so that her doctor has instructed us to make sure all of Margaret's last wishes are in place while she still has a sound mind. It appears her illness is entering into its final phase. She can only be home alone for very short periods of time, due to her high risk of falling. It is becoming harder for her to breathe. The cumulative effects of her illness have taken their toll. Whether she will live days, months, or years is a mystery. What is no mystery is her body is wearing out.

So now our reality is that each day Margaret has to deal with significant loss of muscle strength, chronic chest and joint pain, abdominal discomfort,

Always Sick, Always Loved

and frequent fatigue. To navigate our home she must walk very cautiously with the assistance of a walker. In order to leave our home, she has to be in a wheelchair. Supplemental oxygen is required twenty-four hours a day. This incurable disease persists in its cruel advancement, and there is little we can do. It continues to give us a life with a steady theme of health challenges. Her physical symptoms pound her body and at times wear her down emotionally. Her medications provide some relief, but also give her side effects that range from sleepiness to nausea. Apart from a miracle, her illness will likely take her life within the next year or so. It is a quarter-century long battle we would not wish on anyone.

So why have we shared all of these details about our "bitter pill of chronic illness?" Our goal is not to get your pity. It is simply to let you know that this has been our reality. It is not a reality without God's love. It is a reality experienced *with* God's love. You see, our experience is not unique. Millions of people live in similar circumstances today. From the crippling afflictions in the later years to catastrophic injuries or disabilities in the younger years, many of us are called to live with pain. Countless others are destined to live with and care for those who are suffering. The patient may be very young, very old, or somewhere in between. The need for care may last for a few days, or it may carry on for several years. Regardless of the duration, will you and I experience the power and comfort of God? Is God's love so great that even with an illness or disability a person can experience peace, hope, and joy? If apathy and bitterness have gripped your soul, can the Lord transform your heart into one of gratefulness? Is

"The Bitter Pill of Chronic Illness"

it possible to have to care for a sick loved one and still look at your life as blessed by God? In other words, is the power of the gospel so amazing that a family can endure decades of chronic disease and still grow in their love for God and their love for each other?

Well, these are some of the questions we are going to address, so welcome to our journey. Please read on prayerfully, and discover God's means of giving persevering power and hope through years of chronic disease.

Discussion Questions

1) Describe the history and details of your current health-related challenge.
2) What are the most difficult things you have to deal with?
3) As you think about your situation, what are the most significant struggles you have in your relationship with God?

Chapter Two

"The Gospel and Chronic Disease"

"Now I would remind you, brothers, of the gospel I preached to you, which you received, in which you stand, and by which you are being saved... For I delivered to you as of first importance what I also received: that Christ died for our sins in accordance with the Scriptures, that he was buried, [and] that he was raised on the third day in accordance with the Scriptures" (1 Corinthians 15:1,3-4).

Though I hope all the chapters of our book are beneficial to you, I would designate this chapter by far as the most significant. For in the more than twenty years we have dealt with Margaret's chronic illness, without a doubt the most impacting message of hope and strength has been (and still is) the gospel of Jesus Christ. Without the reality of Jesus in our lives, I shudder to think where we would be today.

"The Gospel and Chronic Disease"

Yet as I begin to write about the amazing benefits we have received via the gospel, my heart aches. The weightiness in my spirit comes as I think about all the confusion swirling around the glorious message of the gospel as it relates to chronic illness. Sadly, a currently popular position in some Christian circles is that faith in Christ and chronic disease cannot coexist with each other. To summarize, this message makes these kinds of declarations: "If God has transformed a person through trusting in Jesus Christ, then it is never God's will for him or her to be physically ill. Didn't faith lead to miraculous healings in Jesus' day? Therefore, if your walk with God is strong, your expectation should be to experience Jesus' healing miracles as well. All sickness is from the devil. You are a child of the king. It is never God's will for you to be sick, let alone stay sick."

I think most of us facing medical trials have seen the judgmental looks, and have heard the Bible-backed hurtful comments. Folks questioning the real cause of our troubles—trying to pinpoint a spiritual deficiency that is the root cause of why disease and disability have planted themselves into our lives. In this context the words of Jesus have not brought us hope. Rather, we have felt the sting of judgment, a sense of failure, and have been provoked to introspective condemnation.

In light of the confusion that exists, I am grateful to be able to share how the gospel of Christ is our life-changing, transforming message of hope even in the darkest moments of our medical journey. I am excited to say that when God draws you to the Savior, your heart and perspective can be transformed through his loving power. Your health circumstances may stay the same or get worse—yet your soul can be on a path of rejuvenation through the gospel. Margaret and I continue to live in the goodness of the gospel—with a moment-by-moment companion of disease. Her illness doesn't mean we are failing God. Rather, we have the opportunity to experience God's love in a special and profound way.

Here are a few questions I would challenge you with if you or someone you love has a chronic health condition: Do you doubt God loves you? Do you wonder if you have somehow failed God, and are now getting what you deserve? Do you feel God is punishing you for some mysterious sin, or for your lack of faith? Are you bitter and angry toward God for giving you such a challenge? Do you think you deserve better in this life, and do you feel God has not been fair to you and your family? Do you long for a fresh start, hoping to realize anew God's comfort, and the realization that he is with you in your medical troubles?

If you answered "yes" to any of these questions, I would encourage you to prayerfully consider what you are about to read. The truth is that I have answered "yes" to those questions numerous times over the years. One such example involves harboring anger at the Lord. On some Sunday mornings I would worship, pray, and act like I loved God. On the inside, however, I seriously doubted his love for me and my family, and was upset at him for our medical trials. I wondered how a loving God and Savior would allow the ongoing health struggles we were facing. After all, how could a God of love let a wonderful woman like Margaret suffer so severely? Shouldn't our faith and righteous life be rewarded by health, prosperity, and needed miracles? Why did Jesus heal people during his ministry here on

"The Gospel and Chronic Disease"

earth, but yet for some mysterious reason he won't allow Margaret to be healed?

During these times when I struggled with bitterness and with seeing God's love for us, I knew that if we were to endure the rough road of chronic disease, we needed a strength that exceeded human determination. We had to have a supernatural strength and a truth-based vision for our lives that went way beyond a healing miracle. We needed a hope that would sustain us even if our sarcoidosis challenges got worse. Here are some of the questions I seriously asked myself: "Does the gospel give hope to those imprisoned within the walls of chronic disease? Is there a miraculous, inner freedom that God can provide to those chained by a life-long disability? Can families rocked by a severe illness see the power of God in their lives? How does the gospel apply to those faced with crippling afflictions?"

Well, the good news is that the gospel can bring hope to those in hopeless medical conditions. By his mercy, we have experienced his transforming power no matter how difficult our circumstances have been. There is so much to say on this topic, but I'd like to begin by looking into what the biblical message of the gospel is.

<u>What is the Gospel?</u>

"For the Son of Man came to seek and to save the lost" (Luke 19:10).

When our children were very young, we loved to read to them from a book called *The Gospel for Children* by John B. Leuzarder. In the simplest yet most profound way, the author states, "Gospel means good news."[4] Good news—it is what everyone wants to hear. When life's troubles hit us hard, we need good news that gives us hope. This hope can't be in a favorable ending to our difficulties. Real-life often does not play out like a feel-good movie. A disease hits a loved one, progresses, and we watch gradual and often irreversible physical deterioration. Chances are there will not be the classic storybook ending. With an illness, people don't typically live life happily ever after. They live a challenging life characterized by pain, fatigue, and a host of medically related obstacles. Sick people and their families need a much deeper, real hope that goes light years beyond a change in circumstances. They need hope-filled news that only the Creator of the universe can provide. It is a deep-seated hope of the heart, based on the teachings of the Bible. It is the rooted assurance that though my body may be breaking down, my spirit grows stronger in knowing God loves me and cares for me. This kind of hope is only found in the gospel.

Simply stated, to experience God's love and comfort in a deep way we must have a relationship with him. Thankfully we don't have to rely on our own ability to create this relationship. Jesus said, "No one can come to me unless the Father who sent me draws him" (John 6:44). He also said, "I am the way, and the truth, and the life. No one comes to the Father except through me" (John 14:6). The relationship that the Lord desires to have with you is initiated by him. Do you sense his voice inviting you to draw near to him? Do you have a yearning in your heart to be close to Christ? Respond to the Lord. Humble yourself before him and talk to God about your deepest needs. The ultimate

"The Gospel and Chronic Disease"

bad news is that our sins have separated us from God. Consequently we are under his holy and righteous judgment. Jesus came to remedy our sin problem. He lived, died, and rose again so you and I could experience his love, and have the promise of eternal life with him. Here is the important question we must all answer: Do I know the Savior? Do I have peace with God through Christ Jesus our Lord?

I think adversity, whether medical or otherwise, can either drive us to God or embitter our hearts away from him. My prayer is that your family's health challenges will be used by God to encourage you to seek him. He is the giver of love, hope, forgiveness and comfort. Do you know him?

My first encounter with God came when I was in high school. As a seventeen-year-old senior, I seldom (if ever) thought about the Lord. I was a "good kid," trying to please my parents and working to do my best in school. I also had a love for most sports, but with my shoulder length hair resting on the top of my 5'8" 120-pound frame, I was never skilled or physically strong enough to make a high school team. (Let's just say the words "tryout" and "cut" were inseparably linked in my experience—I tried out, and a few days later I got cut—a cycle which repeated itself a number of times in my "stellar" sports career.) Then in December of 1976 I heard the varsity bowling team was holding open tryouts. (Yes, my high school had a bowling team—a long-standing tradition in the damp upstate New York winters.) Since they were being held at Midway Lanes, a place I had bowled numerous times, I felt like I had a kind of home court advantage. I also knew this would probably be my last chance to earn a varsity letter.

Always Sick, Always Loved

The night before the tryouts began, I couldn't fall asleep. I kept picturing in my mind how tomorrow's bowling events would play out. I visualized myself methodically taking my four-step approach. I saw the release of my dark blue bowling ball from my right hand, staring it down as it spun about four inches from the right gutter. Then I saw the ball make the sharp left turn into the pins, resulting in an explosive strike. Yet as I continued in my bowling fantasy, I also started talking to myself. "These moments of sports greatness could happen, couldn't they? Surely I have a shot, don't I?" Then the reality side of my brain kicked in, bringing with it waves of adolescent despair. "Who am I kidding?" I thought. "Another tryout, and get ready for another cut. It would take a miracle for you to make the team."

If you are wondering where this is leading, this was the context for one of the first prayers I ever uttered. Sure, adolescent athletic hopelessness may seem like a miniscule trial at best, but at the time I felt deep desperation. I knew I needed help that far exceeded my natural ability. So, lying on my bed that winter night I meekly started talking to the Lord. My prayer sounded something like this: "God, if you are out there, I would really appreciate your help tomorrow in the bowling tryouts. Please help me so I can get a varsity letter before I graduate. Amen."

Little did I know that when I started my warm-up tosses at 4:00 p.m. the next afternoon I would witness my first specific answer to a prayer. Amazingly, my first three games had me on top of the leader board with an average of almost 210 pins per game. Two days later, I completed the nine-game competition in the top seven.

"The Gospel and Chronic Disease"

I had made the team, and, more importantly, had experienced my own personal "miracle on the lanes."

My bowling "miracle" deeply impressed on my heart that God really did exist. Not only did I think he was real, but I also saw he did in fact care about me. A few months later, to my total surprise, a classmate shared the gospel with me. Here I was, completing my last few weeks at Vestal Senior High School, and now I hear about Jesus. God showed himself to me on the lanes, and now he was speaking to me at school. I couldn't escape him. Things were happening, and for the first time in my life I gave some serious thought to the person of Jesus Christ. What was the Lord trying to show me? Did the Savior really love me? Was the answer to my prayer at Midway Lanes just a taste of what he wanted to do in my life?

A few weeks later I drove to a local bookstore and purchased my first Bible. It was a tan-colored paperback containing the New Testament and Psalms. I began to read and reread the Gospel of John, the book of Romans, and the book of Ephesians. I can still recall the heavy weight of guilt I felt (I'd call this understanding the "bad" news) as I read these key verses:

- "For all have sinned and fall short of the glory of God" (Romans 3:23).

- "For the wages of sin is death, but the free gift of God is eternal life in Christ Jesus our Lord" (Romans 6:23).

- "For by grace you have been saved through faith. And this is not your own doing; it is the

Always Sick, Always Loved

gift of God, not a result of works, so that no one may boast" (Ephesians 2:8-9).

I began to realize my sin had left me under God's righteous judgment. I started to see that no matter how good I tried to be, I could never be good enough. I knew I was eternally doomed. I needed Jesus to come and take away my sins. I needed his forgiveness, based on his completed work on the cross. How incredible it was for me to then begin to understand the good news of the gospel! Here are some of the key verses that pointed me to faith in Christ:

• "For God so loved the world, that he gave his only Son, that whoever believes in him should not perish, but have eternal life. For God did not send his Son into the world to condemn the world, but in order that the world might be saved through him" (John 3:16-17).

• "Because, if you confess with your mouth that Jesus is Lord and believe in your heart that God raised him from the dead, you will be saved. For with the heart one believes and is justified, and with the mouth one confesses and is saved" (Romans 10:9-10).

Weeks later, on a humid night in July of 1977, I found myself listening to a preacher at Montrose Bible Conference in Montrose, Pennsylvania. During the message it felt as if I was the only person there. It was as if I was hearing the Lord singling me out, calling me by name. As the speaker preached the gospel, I was

"The Gospel and Chronic Disease"

gripped with the reality that without Jesus I was going to face God's eternal judgment in hell. I knew I needed Jesus to forgive me of all my sins.

Shortly after the message, while sitting in my algae green 1971 Plymouth Duster, I prayed to ask Christ to be my Savior and forgive me of all my sins. My prayer was nothing special or eloquent. It went something like this: "Lord, I realize I have sinned against you. I understand because of my sin I am under your holy judgment. But now I ask you, Jesus, to save me from my sins. I believe you are God, that you died on the cross for my sins, and that you rose again three days later. I put my total trust in you to save me and forgive me. Amen."

That night I clearly understood for the first time Jesus was God in the flesh, and he died a horrible death on the cross for my sins. He took God's penalty for my sins so I wouldn't have to. Three days later he rose from the dead, proving to the world that he was the Son of God. After putting my faith in Christ, for the first time in my life I knew God had forgiven all my sins, and I had no doubt that when I died I would go to heaven and be with him.

The peace and excitement I felt in my heart that night was real and life changing. In the days ahead some of my closest friends thought I was going through a new fad, entering into my Jesus phase. They figured in a few months I would move on to something else. Yet—thank God—despite all my spiritual ups and downs over the years, I can honestly say today that I love Jesus, and thank God for his love and mercy in my life. Sure, I still have my faults and failures, and am in frequent need of his forgiveness and help. But that night in 1977 he changed the course of my life forever. He made me his child, and initiated my Christian journey. I was given a new birth, a wonderful new beginning in Christ.

This is the gospel of Christ. We all need to understand our sins have separated us from God, and the payment for those sins is God's holy judgment. We are spiritually dead and without hope in this world. The good news is that Jesus came to save us from our sins. Praise God—Jesus came, died, rose again, and now provides the way to have a personal relationship with him. Look again at Jesus' words in John 14:6: "I am the way, and the truth, and the life. No one comes to the Father except through me." By faith we must receive his gift of salvation. We must realize our hopeless state before him, and put our total trust in what Christ has done. Then the miracle of a new life begins. As I once heard said, "God takes you out of the courtroom and puts you into his family room." Yes, as a Christian, you are now his child, with a glorious inheritance of eternal life through Jesus Christ our Lord.

Salvation in Christ is the first and most pivotal step in experiencing God's hope and comfort. Maybe the time has come for you to take a personal soul inventory. Is God tugging at your heart to take a serious look at your life, and your relationship with him? Do you know you have eternal life in Christ? Are you sure your sins are forgiven by his blood? Have your circumstances pressed you to the point of hopelessness, so much so that you are deeply discouraged, and embittered toward God? Ask the Lord to give you the real hope and encouragement that only comes from Jesus. Ask God to help you turn from your sins, and come freshly to him. A new beginning can come to your life through the gospel of Christ. As the scriptures say,

"The Gospel and Chronic Disease"

"Therefore, if anyone is in Christ, he is a new creation. The old has passed away; behold, the new has come" (2 Corinthians 5:17).

Thankfully, the gospel is so much more than just knowing heaven awaits me at the point of my death. The gospel also gives real hope in the darkest times of difficulty. Note the words of Jerry Bridges:

> This good news doesn't begin when we die. It certainly does address that issue, but it also tells us there is good news for us now. We don't have to feel guilt-ridden and insecure in our relationship with God. We don't have to wonder if He likes us. We can begin each day with the deeply encouraging realization that I am accepted by God, not on the basis of my personal performance, but on the basis of the infinitely perfect righteousness of Jesus Christ.[5]

This is what I will address in the remainder of this chapter. I hope and pray that if you are chronically ill, or care for someone who is, you will experience the good news for you *now*. The gospel can daily (if not moment by moment) encourage you in so many ways. I'd like to begin by looking at how the gospel can deepen your realization of God's love for you.

The Assurance of God's Love

"But God shows his love for us in that while we were still sinners, Christ died for us" (Romans 5:8).

Always Sick, Always Loved

Some of my fondest childhood memories involve airplanes. When I was around twelve my dad decided he wanted to get his private pilot's license. After hours of rigorous in-flight and classroom training, Dad earned his "wings" and then airborne excursions became a frequent part of my family's life.

One of these excursions, particularly for my brother and me, was the breakfast commute at 9000 feet. During summer weekends, we'd often receive a wake-up call around 6:00 a.m. The deep-voiced words, "Come on boys, let's head down to the airport and go out to breakfast," was an invitation we couldn't refuse. I clearly recall seeing my father standing in the room I shared with my brother, eager to rouse his sons to experience the day's aviation adventure. His attire also communicated the theme of the morning: a tan flying jacket cloaked his upper body; dark, wire-rimmed glasses shaded his cool blue eyes; and a set of maps were grasped firmly in his right hand. He was clearly the pilot, eager to be airborne, and we were his designated passengers. Time was of the essence, so in haste we got out of bed, threw on some clothes, and piled ourselves into the car.

After the short drive to the airport, my dad thoroughly completed his preflight checks, and with the words "Clear prop, contact," he fired up the single-engine aircraft. Within a few minutes we were rolling down runway two-one, lifting off on our way to some unknown diner at some remote upstate New York airport.

When the sleek, white Cessna 182 landed, we would walk into the airport restaurant and enjoy a tasty hot breakfast, usually of the eggs and bacon variety. All was

"The Gospel and Chronic Disease"

good, fun, and adventuresome—unless of course the weather decided to change while we were eating. Then the calm predictability of our flight home morphed into more of an amusement park ride with sudden twists, turns, and jolts. Laughter and a pleasant sense of breakfast fullness turned to fearful looks and a search for an airsickness bag—just in case. With the unexpected arrival of bumpy air and limited visibility, my stomach found itself seriously pondering whether it should reject its recently consumed eggs, bacon, and toast.

On these rough weather days, the scariest moments for me were always when we flew into clouds. In seconds our aircraft was swallowed into a sea of white. I couldn't see the ground. I couldn't see the sun. All I could see was a panicky look in my brother's eyes, and my father staring intently at the control panel. He had often told me how easy it was to get disorientated in heavy "soup," and how vital it was to believe the readings of the gauges in front of him. "If you don't pay attention," he would say, "you could be upside down and not even know it." Needless to say, great relief came to me when we broke out of the clouds and saw blue sky and bright sunshine. (And we were still right side up.) Yes, all was well outside of cloud-ville, even if the wind still rocked the plane a bit and there were a few more air miles to travel before we got home.

I think living in a chronic illness world is a lot like flying in clouds. The positive, good outlook on our lives can be swallowed up by the storms of our medical trials. Our spiritual orientation can be lost. We can seriously begin to wonder if God truly loves us. The medical storm is so intense we cannot tell where we are headed. All we can see are the clouds of our trial, and

Always Sick, Always Loved

the concerned looks of those around us. We wonder if we can survive, or if we will come out of our challenges so flipped upside down in our souls that we will inevitably crash and burn. We thought God loved us, but now everything is so difficult that it is increasingly hard to know his love still shines on us. If only we could really see the Son in the middle of our medical clouds. Is there a way to know for certain God loves us during these difficult times?

Thankfully, the answer to this question is a resounding "Yes!" The deep assurance of God's love is found in the gospel. He loved us while we were still sinners, living in rebellion against him (note again Romans 5:8). Once we are saved through faith in Christ, he promises he will never leave us or forsake us. We are eternally secure in his love. Nothing can separate us from the love of Christ. Note these incredible verses found in Romans 8:

> Who shall separate us from the love of Christ? Shall tribulation, or distress, or persecution, or famine, or nakedness, or danger, or sword?... No, in all these things we are more than conquerors through him who loved us. For I am sure that neither death nor life, nor angels or rulers, nor things present nor things to come, nor powers, nor height nor depth, nor anything else in all creation, will be able to separate us from the love of God in Christ Jesus our Lord (Romans 8:35,37-39).

God has given us a "control panel" to be reassured of his love; that spiritual set of gauges is his word, and

"The Gospel and Chronic Disease"

more specifically is his gospel. When life's problems bombard our souls, what will keep us on course, safe and secure in the reality of his love, is the gospel of Christ. Yet what I have found is that to keep the gospel before me requires a purposeful, intense level of concentration. The living medical reality before me shouts very loudly to my soul that God doesn't love me. Pain, suffering, and medical hardship don't naturally stir me to thank the Lord for his love for me and my family. So, to keep the right perspective of God's love requires purposeful action. I must talk to myself over and over again, reminding my soul of the Lord's eternal, unchanging love for me.

When Margaret was hospitalized in August of 2005, for the first time cancer was listed as a possible diagnosis. Hearing the "C" word was a cloud of trouble I had never anticipated. Our kids were only eight and ten. After so many years of health challenges, the prospect of possibly losing Margaret to cancer was crushing.

One night, driving home from the hospital, I was really struggling. My mind drifted to the many reasons I thought God didn't love us. Here's a sample of my negative thoughts: "Margaret loves you, Lord, and now she may die of cancer. I love you, Lord, and now it looks like you may leave me a widower with two young children. She suffers so much and she is your child. Yet I see so many people that could care less about you, and they can do whatever they want. Their bodies are healthy and strong, and they never darken the door of a church. We try to serve you with our lives, and we keep getting pounded by health problems."

Then things went from bad to worse as I stopped at a red light. A rusty old pick-up truck pulled up next to me, music blaring, with two very gruff passengers cursing and laughing. As I took a long look at the men next to me, all I could think of was one word: *Unfair.* "Yes, Lord, our situation is not fair. Think about it— Margaret, the godliest woman I know, lies in a hospital bed, grimacing with searing lung pain every time she takes a breath. Next to me are Joe and Jim Obnoxious, men who use your name in vain with every breath, and they ride around free as can be. How can you say you love us when things are going like this?"

Mercifully, on this sad summer night, God began to speak to my soul. What I did over the next few minutes I would encourage anyone to do when trouble distorts your understanding of God's love. Talk to yourself about the gospel. Tell yourself you know God loves you because of what Jesus did for you on the cross. Be purposeful and proactive with the gospel message. As someone well said, "preach the gospel to yourself."[6]

As the old pick-up left the intersection, my downward inner spiral was about to end. All my negative thoughts were soon put on hold by an internal conversation I started to have based on biblical truth. I sensed the Lord bring John 3:16 to my mind. I first took a few seconds to ponder the verse: "For God so loved the world, that he gave his only Son, that whoever believes in him should not perish but have eternal life."

Then my internal dialog escalated. "Mike, how do you know God loves you?" I asked myself. Sheepishly I responded. "Because Jesus died on the cross for my sins." The feebleness in my response provoked me to talk some more. "That was weak. How do you know God loves you? Say it like you mean it!" At this point I began to repeat John 3:16 out loud, over and over again. I'm not sure how many times I said the verse, but I know it was a steady progression of decibels—each time a bit louder, each time with more conviction. Within minutes I was actually shouting John 3:16 inside my red Geo. More importantly, my feelings of doom, gloom, and unfairness were displaced by a fresh realization of God's love through the gospel.

As crazy as you may think my moments in the car were, I think the fruit speaks for itself. It is also a practice I continue to try to cultivate each and every day. Sure, I may not always be shouting verses inside my car, but in my soul I strive to keep the gospel message loud and clear.

The reason I know God loves me is because Christ's death on the cross was the greatest act of love ever seen. God's unconditional love is not based on my circumstances. It is not based on my performance. It is based on what Jesus did at Calvary. So, as a Christian, I find great comfort and encouragement through dwelling on what Christ did for me. Ponder these words written by John Piper:

> The death of Christ is not only the demonstration of *God's* love (John 3:16), it is also the supreme expression of *Christ's own* love for those who receive it as their treasure. The early witnesses who suffered most for being Christians were captured by this fact: Christ "loved me and gave himself for me" (Galatians 2:20). They took the self-giving act of Christ's sacrifice very personally. They said, "He loved *me*. He gave himself for *me*. Surely this is the way we should understand the sufferings and

death of Christ. They have to do with me. They are about Christ's love for me personally.[7]

Have your medical challenges depleted your soul? Do you frequently think God doesn't love you because of the hardships that come with sickness and disease? Prayerfully determine to think about the gospel. Say the gospel out loud. As a believer, reassure your heart of God's love for you and your family. He died for you. His love for you is eternal, and nothing can separate you from his love. It is completely based on what he has done. The reality is that the Son is shining above your medical clouds of trouble, and, he promises to love you and be with you during every moment of your medical trial. What a Savior! What amazing love he has shown through the death, burial, and resurrection of Christ Jesus our Lord!

Incredibly, there is so much more encouragement to be found in the gospel. Let's now look at how God can also free us from the heavy weight of condemnation.

Freedom from Condemnation

"There is therefore now no condemnation for those who are in Christ Jesus" (Romans 8:1).

In the course of writing this book, I have often wondered how many times those who are chronically ill struggle with condemnation. What I mean by condemnation is self-imposed guilt. You blame yourself for your affliction. You think the reason for your medical trial is *you*. You must be doing something wrong, for surely the cause of your pain is God's judgment and

"The Gospel and Chronic Disease"

punishment. If you are the parent of a disabled child, you may wonder what you did (or didn't do) to keep your child from being healthy. If you are a sick mother, you may often wonder if God is nailing you for a lack of gratefulness, or some other yet-to-be-revealed sin. As a caregiver, you may be convinced that God has mapped out your hard road to discipline you for some sin of your youth.

In addition to our self-imposed condemnation, sometimes critical and cutting words come from others. These judgmental comments are painful to take, and are often dogmatic in nature. Here's a summary of comments we've heard, particularly in the first few years Margaret was ill: "It is never God's will you are sick. This illness is all in your head. You need to seek God, find out what your sin is, and repent. Then you will be healed. Don't give in to the sickness. Stand on God's word, confess his promises and you will be healed. If you had more faith, you would experience the healing you long for."

Related to this are comments that attempt to give a behavioral reason for the affliction. These comments sound like this: "The reason Margaret is sick is because she drank diet cola as a teenager. You deserve your disease because you didn't exercise enough. Remember all the coffee you drank in the summer of 1987? Well, you are just reaping what you sowed."

Pardon the use of a math term—but as a math teacher I can't resist—all these comments have a common denominator: the reason for your chronic illness is *you*. You messed up, you don't have enough faith, you didn't follow God the way you should have, and on and on it goes. Are you sick because of your own personal sin? Is your family member ill because of her insufficient faith? Is the hospitalized child battling chronic health issues because of a mom or dad's sin? Conversely, are people healthy and strong because they have a level of faith which protects them from injury and disease? Are they super saints who have attained something I haven't learned to reach? Have they had such superb health habits that their bodies are now protected from disease and disabilities?

I will look more closely at these questions in a few moments when I dig into John 9, but first, I think it is important to clarify a key point related to condemnation: the contrast between condemnation and the conviction of sin. Conviction of sin is neither self-initiated, nor self-imposed, nor is it the judgmental message brought by others. Conviction of sin comes from the Holy Spirit. It is God's work in our hearts. The goal of the Spirit's conviction is to point us to the Savior. Jesus said, in reference to the coming of the Holy Spirit, "When he comes, he will convict the world concerning sin and righteousness and judgment: concerning sin, because they do not believe in me" (John 16:8-9).

For example, in the weeks before I became a Christian, I was convicted of my sin and rebellion against God. I knew in my heart that I had sinned against the Lord, and was destined to face his righteous judgment. I knew I was "condemned," sentenced to an eternity without Christ because of my own sin. This motivated me to turn to Jesus. It pointed me to the only place to find true forgiveness and redemption. My conviction brought me to a place of seeking God and putting my total hope in Christ.

"The Gospel and Chronic Disease"

In the years since I became a believer, there have been countless times when I knew by my actions and attitudes I had sinned against God. The Lord has lovingly helped me realize that what I did was sin against him and others. This conviction also pointed me to the forgiveness of the Savior. It reminded me that I am helpless without him, that only he can forgive me of my sins and restore the joy of my salvation (note Psalm 51). What I have experienced (and it is the biblical pattern as well) is that the Spirit's conviction is specific, and always directs me to Christ. It is not ambiguous or mysterious, and does not put me on a path of morbid vague introspection. "The purpose of the Holy Spirit is not condemnation but conviction of the need for the Savior."[8]

God's conviction is good, loving, and beneficial, because it directs a soul to Jesus. Condemnation is hurtful, destructive, and man-centered. Instead of lovingly reminding a person of their need for a Savior, it puts both the blame for their ills and the responsibility for remedying them on the individual. Condemnation breeds hopelessness and despair. Conviction yields forgiveness, hope and restoration. So, we need to respond to the conviction the Holy Spirit brings to us. We need to reject the voice and bondage of condemnation.

Now let's dig into the words of Jesus. Note this amazing passage of Scripture in John 9:1-3, verses I would classify as "condemnation breakers:"

As he passed by, he saw a man blind from birth. And his disciples asked him, "Rabbi, who sinned, this man or his parents, that he was born blind?" Jesus answered, "It was not that this man sinned, or his parents, but that the works of God might be displayed in him."

The first thing I find quite interesting in this passage is how the disciples want to make a spiritual connection to the man's blindness. Using clear cause-and-effect logic, they ask Jesus to identify who is to blame. It is a multiple-choice question with only two choices: the man or his parents. In other words, a son's disability must be caused by his own sin or his parents' sin. There are no other explanations. Isn't this how we and those around us often think? In our case, does Margaret have sarcoidosis because she sinned, I sinned, or her parents sinned? In your mind, do you wonder if these are your primary reasons why you or someone you love is ill? Condemnation is always ready to point the finger at you, and spew its bile into your heart. Be ready to attack these condemning accusations with the power of the gospel.

How I thank God for Jesus' response. "It was *not* that this man sinned, or his parents, but that the works of God might be displayed in him" (emphasis mine). Let the emphasized word grip your soul. The man's blindness was *not* caused by his specific sin. It was *not* caused by his parents' sin. Rather, God allowed it to display his work. (God's will and purpose with chronic disease is something that will be discussed in the next chapter—the key point here is how the cause of the man's affliction is not linked to a specific sin.)

What freedom this brings from condemnation! Because of what Christ has done for you, the penalty for all your sins has been paid. He is not beating you up physically because of some unrevealed sin. You and

"The Gospel and Chronic Disease"

your family are not being judged due to your spiritual deficiencies. His mysterious plan for your life happens to include a chronic illness or disability. The goal is not to make you feel condemned and under his judgment. Rather, it is to see the works of God in your life. Like the blind man, he may bring healing. Or, according to his plan, he may show his works through years of faith-empowered perseverance. No matter what the medical outcome, you are free from condemnation because of Christ's love for you.

As much as we'd like to think otherwise, being born into this world will bring to each of us everything mortality has to offer. We are born with a frail human body. If we live long enough, we will see the steady decline of our physical strength. The truth is, in this sinful, fallen world, we face the inevitable prospect of disease, disability, and pain. No one can avoid it. Even the godliest of people age, develop chronic health issues, and eventually die. So, medical challenges in our lives should not come to us as a surprise. Nor should the arrival of afflictions stir in us a load of condemnation. You and I are mortal creatures living in a fallen world. Sickness and suffering come to us in the natural course of life on this planet.

Are there any health conditions that can be linked to a specific sin or behavior? How about the IV drug user who contracts HIV? How about the man who drives home drunk and hits a tree, leaving him paralyzed for life? How about the chain-smoker who has been diagnosed with lung cancer? Aren't these and a host of other afflictions rightfully linked to poor life choices? Shouldn't people who get sick because of their own unhealthy lifestyles rightfully feel condemned?

Yes, there are some ailments that certainly can be linked to sinful acts or behavioral choices. Still, God wants his people in these circumstances to experience his forgiveness through the gospel of Christ. Jesus died for all our sins. His blood also cleanses us from all unrighteousness. Here again is the power of the gospel. If you are blaming yourself for your affliction, God wants to comfort you with his forgiving power. There is no condemnation in Christ. Jesus forgives the man who confesses his sin of drug abuse. He can redeem the person who drove home drunk and is now disabled in a wheelchair. What he did on the cross is more powerful than any sin we have done. Come to him, put your total trust in Christ, and experience his freedom from condemnation.

As I conclude this section, I would like to also encourage all of you who are caregivers. Taking care of a chronically ill loved one brings a host of challenges. If you are like me, it also frequently reveals a bunch of sinful attitudes. I would love to say I usually respond appropriately when Margaret is suffering and needs my care. Sadly there are still many times when this is not the case. I particularly struggle when she needs my help in the middle of the night. Interrupted sleep tends to really reveal my sin.

I remember a few years ago when I had one of my 2:00 a.m. caregiver wake-up calls. Very early on a Thursday morning I was awakened by a dull groaning sound. Margaret's sarcoidosis ankle pain had again reared its ugly head, and most of her joints followed her ankle's lead. She was grimacing in severe pain, trying to muffle the sound so as not to wake me. As I left the land of peaceful sleep for the late-night world

"The Gospel and Chronic Disease"

of medical care, I was not a happy husband. While she sat next to me, tearfully and apologetically telling me of her pain, internally I was fuming. My tone toward her was harsh. My primary concern was how this wake-up call was going to affect me. In less than six hours, I was supposed to be cheerfully teaching my first hour math class. How in the world was I supposed to do my job if I was up most of night with her? Margaret could tell I was annoyed at the situation. Her eyes looked into mine with a justified perplexity. Why was I being so rude to her for being sick?

After I helped her down the stairs to our living room recliner, I sat at our kitchen table, my head in my hands, weakly asking God what I should do. His Spirit of conviction came. I knew I had sinned against the Lord and Margaret. My selfish sinful attitude had added emotional pain to her physical suffering. I felt like a piece of dirt. In fact, I felt lower than dirt. I thought, "Mike, you jerk. How can you be so selfishly rude toward Margaret, especially when she is in so much pain?" In my sleep-deprived state, the waves of guilt immobilized me. Yet Margaret still needed my comfort and care. Her pain intensified. What was I going to do?

Thankfully as I sat there paralyzed by condemnation, the Lord reminded me of the cross. I thought of his love for me. I reminded myself of the reality of his death for my sins. I confessed my sin to him. I thanked him for forgiving me. I then experienced his peace. Guilt was replaced by hope for the day. He helped me lift my head out of my hands and to begin to pray for her. I also began to pray for wisdom. Mercifully, I saw what I needed to do: confess my sin to Margaret, call in to request a substitute teacher, and get a doctor's appointment for her as soon as possible. Incredibly, despite my early a.m. sins, the day came together in a way where all our needs were provided for.

Without the gospel to free me from my guilt and condemnation, this day probably would have turned out much differently. Maybe our practical needs would have been met, but a cloud of guilt and remorse would have hung over me the entire day. Thank God for the blood of Jesus that washes away all our sins. Thank God again for the power of the cross.

Can you relate to my sinful attitudes? Have you ever gotten angry at your sick loved one? Do you see more failures in your role as a caregiver than successes? Have you so much bitterness and resentment in your soul that you feel you'd win the award for the "Biggest Loser as a Caregiver?" I can relate. I can also say the most important thing to do now is look to Jesus. Preach the gospel to yourself over and over again. He forgives you and wants to give you fresh hope for today.

Sick or well, the gospel is the power of God for salvation to all who believe (see 1 Corinthians 1:18). At the foot of the cross there is plenty of room for people suffering from disease, in wheelchairs, and with a host of other afflictions. There is also plenty of room for all those who provide their needed practical care. Knowing the Savior's love and forgiveness is vital in persevering through the days, months, or years of chronic disease.

You see, the gospel is the reason why this book is being written. All the wonderful blessings we have received in the midst of chronic illness all find their way back to the cross. Any good thing I have been able to do as a husband in caring for Margaret is because of what Jesus has done for me. I am still very prone to sin.

"The Gospel and Chronic Disease"

I have to repent often. Nevertheless, the love of Christ demonstrated by his atoning death frees me from my guilt. His eternal love gives us hope for the future. This leads me to another key benefit I've found in preaching the gospel to myself.

Truth-Based Expectations

"For the wages of sin is death, but the free gift of God is eternal life in Christ Jesus our Lord" (Romans 6:23).

In just a few weeks I will be starting my twenty-eighth consecutive year as a high school math teacher. One of my favorite days of the school year is the first day of school. My students typically enter my classroom on day one looking well-groomed and wide-eyed, with expressions which range from excitement to complete dread. I hear comments like: "Are *you* my Algebra teacher? Is there going to be a seating chart? Do you give homework every day?" Inevitably I'll also hear my personal motivational favorite, "I have never done well in math. In fact, it would be a miracle if I passed this class." Yes, here they are, my new group of math recruits, sentenced to five hours per week in my classroom. Let the math adventure begin!

On the first day of school I usually take over twenty minutes discussing class expectations. This is when my students get the news on each and every "Robble math" classroom policy. I talk about behavior. I discuss required supplies. They hear about homework, tests, quizzes, and anything else grade-related. Also on the agenda are attendance and tardy policies, fire drill procedures, and lock down rules. I talk a lot, while these new students strain to listen and not drift off into a post-summer sleep.

On the lighter side, I also tell my new students a bit about myself. I enjoy sharing with them about Margaret and the kids. I let them know about our travels from New York to Arizona, and then on to Colorado. They hear an overview of my teaching career. Lastly I find it amusing to move on to Robble personality expectations. This part of the speech goes something like this: "I want to also be very clear with you on one of my most significant faults." The puzzled looks begin to emerge. "I believe I am very funny, and possess a comic gift. Therefore, when appropriate, I will not hesitate to share jokes, sound effects, or other comments which I feel have entertainment value." At this point a few students wonder if I have ever had a psychological evaluation. My words continue. "The problem is that few of you will think I am funny. Frankly, I don't care. I will continue in my comic attempts whether or not any of you laugh." Thus their initial exposure to my classroom expectations comes to a close. Day two will start the process of working to establish a daily productive mathematical routine.

As a teacher, I have learned that clear expectations are crucial. Communicating and building beneficial expectations brings stability and calm to my classes. Within a few days a sense of order typically permeates my students. The routine of quickly sitting in their assigned seats, having their homework checked and gone over, and learning new concepts with an abundance of practice becomes our daily ritual of learning. Sure, there are activities that keep us from too much

"The Gospel and Chronic Disease"

predictability. There are also those rare moments when I actually do something that most teens find humorous. Overall, however, they know what to expect from me and what I expect from them. This is Mr. Robble's math world, each weekday at the same time, in the same room, and with the same zany teacher personality.

Want to really upset my students? Bring in a substitute with a totally different set of expectations. Toss the routine out the door. Delete positive learning activities. Add some heavy anger and apathy toward the young adults. Get totally frustrated with a student if he doesn't learn the concept quickly. Change the beneficial expectations, and even the best of students can come unglued.

Outside the confines of a math classroom, it is even more crucial to have realistic, truth-based expectations for our lives. What does God say my normal life is supposed to look like? What routine should I plan to follow on a daily basis? As I reflect on the gospel, what should I anticipate over the years of my life? If our expectations are not based on biblical truth, when things change we will be like my students with a poor substitute teacher. We will freak. We will get angry and frustrated. We will resist fervently all that goes against our expectations. We will find ourselves living in a sea of persistent, discouraging confusion. This is why our expectations in life must be based on the Bible. They must have a solid gospel-centered focus.

What does the Bible say about health expectations? Did Jesus promise physical health alongside our spiritual salvation? Do the scriptures clearly teach all believers in Christ inherit not only eternal life, but also

Always Sick, Always Loved

freedom from sickness? Does God promise to protect us and our children from disease or disabilities?

As I have studied the Bible over the years, what I see is that good health is a blessing from God, but it is not a biblical right. No person or family is given a "trial-free card" regarding physical well-being. We live in a fallen, sinful world. A reality in this fallen world is that people get sick and injured. Sometimes the affliction passes quickly. Sometimes it lasts for years. God may choose to miraculously heal the illness, or he may allow it to remain. We don't have a right to a sickness-free existence. A pain-free life is only promised in heaven.

Ever since Adam and Eve sinned in the Garden of Eden, pain has been a human reality. It is a normal part of our sinful human existence. Studying the life of Jesus, it is very clear he never taught a benefit of following him was a suffering exemption. Dedication to Christ will not protect us from physical infirmities. Look at the example of Jesus. His perfect sinless life ended in his early thirties. He died an excruciating death by crucifixion. God didn't allow him a long, pain-free life. No, in the prime of his life he willingly allowed himself to be executed at the hands of sinful men. As the Bible says, he was "a man of sorrows, and acquainted with grief" (Isaiah 53:3). The scriptures also tell us, "we do not have a high priest who is unable to sympathize with our weaknesses, but one who in every respect has been tempted as we are, yet without sin" (Hebrews 4:15). If Jesus suffered, we too will suffer. Don't believe for a moment that the reward for godliness is a pain-free, wholeness guarantee. It wasn't Jesus' experience, nor will it be ours.

"The Gospel and Chronic Disease"

You may be wondering, "But didn't Jesus heal many people of their diseases and disabilities?" He sure did, but he didn't heal everyone in Israel, nor does he heal everyone today. Reading the accounts of miraculous healings in the Gospels frequently provokes me to pray for Margaret's healing. It can be dangerous, however, to make what Jesus did during his earthly ministry your immovable expectation. Does Jesus have the power to heal today? Yes! Is it his will to heal everyone who is sick or disabled today? No! Why not? I don't know. The answer to that question remains with God. Some today are miraculously healed. Many more are not. As I discussed earlier in this chapter, I don't believe the reason they are not healed is a spiritual deficiency. Rather, their medical outcome is based on God's perfect (and mysterious) will.

When I think about the cross, I am often reminded how merciful God has been to me. Without Jesus I would be hopelessly lost in my sins. I would be facing our daily medical trials without knowledge of God's love for me and my family. If it weren't for the Lord, I would be facing an eternity reaping the consequences for my sins. The reality is that I deserved to fully reap what I had sown. I was hell-bound, without any regard for what pleased God. So in light of what I really deserved, how can I complain if I experience the unavoidable sufferings of this fallen world? Ponder prayerfully the words of D.A. Carson:

> Christians undergoing pain and suffering will be well served by contemplating the Bible's story line and meditating on the price of sin. We live in an age where everyone is concerned about

Always Sick, Always Loved

their "rights." But there is a profound sense in which our "rights" before God have been sacrificed by our sin. If in fact we believe that our sin properly deserves the wrath of God, then when we experience the sufferings of this world, all of them consequences of human rebellion, we will be less quick to blame God and a lot quicker to recognize that we have no fundamental right to expect a life of unbroken ease and comfort. From the biblical perspective, it is of the Lord's mercies that we are not consumed.[9]

The benefits we have received in having biblical, gospel-centered expectations have been life-changing. Steady confusion and questioning of God's plan have been replaced with gratefulness and appreciation for the love of the Savior. Once, we thought Margaret's illness was the consequence of a specific sin or our lack of faith. Now, however, this cloud of condemnation has been cleared by having a more biblically informed understanding of the Lord's forgiveness and mercy. Because of the totality of our sin, our expectation was to face God's righteous judgment. Thanks to Jesus, we are undeservedly redeemed and forever in the family of God.

Despite the intense pain Margaret often feels, the reality is that she and our family are doing amazingly better than we deserve. We could still be objects of God's wrath. We could still be walking in darkness, totally oblivious to God's love and compassion for us. We could all be spiritually dead, without hope, and not knowing God has a plan to use us (and her sarcoidosis) to show his mighty work in us. Think about it. She could

"The Gospel and Chronic Disease"

be physically ill and we could be clueless in our understanding of God's love for us. Life apart from God in the midst of physical suffering is infinitely worse than a life with God in the midst of physical suffering.

This is why, particularly when a chronic affliction is in your family, it is so important to preach the gospel to yourself. (I don't apologize for saying it one more time.) Through Margaret's hours of pain, through nights of interrupted sleep, I have found that my greatest inner comfort has come from reminding myself of God's love for us as shown in the gospel. When God strengthens my heart, I in turn can better encourage her. We were once dead in our sins. Today we are alive in God. We know God loves us. How do we know this? We know this because Jesus went to the cross for our sins, and took God's wrath for us. Today God will help us. How do we know this? Because if Jesus took care of our sin problem, surely he will take care of our daily needs. These are not simple truths to superficially warm our souls in an hour of agony. These are eternal truths that tell our souls God's love is great toward us, even if our physical pain shouts loudly that he doesn't care. Note these words penned by C.J. Mahaney:

> In real life, things do not always go just as we would like. Comfort in suffering can never be found by focusing endlessly on the suffering itself, for suffering always contains an element of impenetrable mystery. Hope and comfort and perseverance in the Christian life come from meditating on the cross and the God of the cross.[10]

Always Sick, Always Loved

In closing this chapter, I think I would be remiss in not discussing one more great benefit that comes through the gospel of Christ. It is the cumulative effect of the assurance of God's love, freedom from condemnation, and truth-based expectations. Yes, even in the most adverse of medical situations, the Lord can keep your soul from bitterness.

The Cure for Bitterness

"See to it that no one fails to obtain the grace of God; that no "root of bitterness" springs up and causes trouble, and by it many become defiled" (Hebrews 12:25).

Over the years, I confess there have been times when I have let the strain of Margaret's illness drive me to a point of despair and hopelessness. During these periods of discouragement I have also found myself getting angry with God. Perceiving our situation to be too big a load for a family to carry, I have either given the Lord the silent treatment, or blatantly told him that our situation was not fair. As I mentioned at the beginning of this chapter, I found myself living a two-faced Christian life: externally I wore the facade of loving and trusting God (my Christian happy face) while internally I stewed with anger and distrust. Mercifully, however, God wouldn't let me stay in this bitterness-infested state for very long. In a personal, loving way he reminded me of what he did for me on the cross. His Spirit convicted me of my sin, and drew me back to the Savior. His love demonstrated at Calvary melted my inner turmoil and gave me gratefulness for all he had

"The Gospel and Chronic Disease"

done for me. This is a miracle of the soul that comes only through the power of the gospel.

Over the years different folks have asked Margaret and me questions like these: "Why aren't you bitter? How can you possibly have joy and thankfulness in your heart in light of all you have been through? Your medical challenges have lasted so long—don't you feel you have a right to be angry and complain to God?" These are great questions. With the longevity and severity of her disease, common sense would say we should wake up each day grumbling, murmuring, and harboring all kinds of angry thoughts toward God. Yet as I write this paragraph, Margaret stands in our kitchen, cooking and singing. Flanked by her walker, and getting added balance with the help of the oven door handle, she stirs potatoes with joy in her heart.

How is this possible? Why isn't she whining, complaining, and showing animosity aimed at the Lord and our family? Has she somehow worked up a happy face? Is this a manufactured joyfulness due to an abundance of human fortitude? On the caregiver side of things, is the peace and contentment I feel in my heart the result of gutsy resolve to not let her illness get the best of me? Have I somehow been given a special dose of caregiver hope due to my strength of character and my personality type? To be sure, both of us are still prone to sin. Neither of us has attained a level of maturity where anger and bitterness issues have been permanently resolved. Yet, by God's mercy, most days we sense hope, peace, joy and gratitude in our hearts. How can this be? The only explanation I can provide is this: it is the miraculous fruit of knowing Christ Jesus our Lord.

For clarity, let's take a closer look at what bitterness is. A definition I like describes it as a state of "exhibiting strong animosity. . . [being] marked by resentment or disappointment."[11] Simply stated, bitterness is anger at God. When I have been bitter, I have concluded that my life is not fair. I have concluded that I have been dealt a hand that I don't deserve. Due to my perceived unfairness of it all, I feel I have a right to be mad at the Lord. After all, my life stinks, and he is to blame. Essentially I pout, whine, and complain. My soul is sick, and I don't care, because I think God deserves rudeness from me. In my mind, the severity of my circumstances justifies my angry attitude.

To make matters worse, bitterness loves company. When I am upset and steaming at God, I usually let it spew out on others. As the scripture at the beginning of this section emphasizes, bitterness "causes trouble, and by it many become defiled." After all, shouldn't I have companions in my misery? Don't I have a right to tell others how unfair the Lord has been to me and my family? When I am affected by bitterness, I want others to agree my life is hard, and to concur with the hardship and confusion our difficulties have caused. In sometimes subtle (or not so subtle) ways, I can entice others to doubt the goodness of God and also have a case for being mad at him on account of me. Pathetically, when I am an angry, resentful, bitter soul, I don't look to encourage others. Rather, I want people to join me in my pit of despair.

I don't apologize for stating again that the only lasting remedy for bitterness of the soul is the life-changing power of the gospel of Christ. Jesus is the "friend who sticks closer than a brother" (Proverbs

"The Gospel and Chronic Disease"

18:24). At times I may desire the company of others who I can vent my misery with, but because I am in Christ, he wants to comfort and encourage me in his love. Since he is my good shepherd, by his power "he restores my soul" (Psalm 23:3). His precious soul restoration transforms me from a bitter man to a thankful man. Fear and distrust is quenched by his assuring words, "I will never leave you nor forsake you" (Hebrews 13:5). Doubts about the dependability of his care are annihilated by the knowledge that he brought full provision to the greatest need I will ever have— being separated from God because of my sins.

As you have read this section, do you see a measure of deep-seated anger in your soul? Like I have, are you harboring resentment toward God and others? Do you long for a supernatural touch from the Lord, a healing of your heart that removes the plague of bitterness and restores to you the joy of your salvation? Come to Christ. Confess your sin of bitterness. Ask him to cleanse you of your sin, and give you a heart of thankfulness, peace, and hope through the love of the Savior. He has done it for us time and time again. Based on the authority of his word, I know he desires to do it for you as well.

In reflecting on the key points of this chapter, my encouragement would be to consistently preach the gospel to yourself. Review daily, if not hourly, what Christ has done for you. Look beyond and above your medical circumstances and see him hanging on the cross for you, and then powerfully rising from the dead. Dwell on his amazing act of unconditional love. Be secure in his eternal unchanging love for you. Meditate on the price he paid to forgive you of your sins. There is no condemnation in Christ. As a Christian, he loves you, died for you, and delights in you. Nothing can separate you from his love.

Also, remember to place your expectations and hopes in his hands. The Lord never promised an easy, sickness-free life. He did promise, however, to love and care for you every step of the way, and show you his amazing love. As these great truths take root in your heart, bitterness will no longer have a place in your life. How can we stay angry with a God who has done so much for us? How can we doubt his love and provision in the midst of our medical difficulties when we understand all he has done to seal our salvation?

I acknowledge in this chapter I have barely scratched the surface of God's glorious gospel. I pray the Lord is stirring in your heart a passion to know him and the gospel in a deeper way. One thing I know is this: without God's love through the gospel of Christ, this book would never have been written. The gospel continues to daily affirm God's love to us. The gospel continues to daily free us from condemnation. The gospel reminds us each day of truth-based expectations for our lives. The gospel guards our hearts from the poison of bitterness. Thank God for his amazing gospel!

Discussion Questions

1. In your own words (and using biblical evidence) explain what the gospel is.

2. If someone were to ask you if you are a Christian, what would you tell them?

"The Gospel and Chronic Disease"

3. Does the reality of the gospel help you face your medical challenges? If so, how? If not, in what ways do you feel you need to be more impacted by the gospel of Christ?

Chapter Three

"A Healthy Doctrine of Suffering"

"If your law had not been my delight, I would have perished in my affliction" (Psalm 119:92).

Sometimes I find it fascinating to observe the dynamic of a TV commercial. Advertisers can be very cunning and creative when trying to convince the watching public of the need for their product. The visual, auditory, and psychological events in just fifteen seconds of airtime can stir us to reach for the car keys and head to the local store.

One of Colorado's largest grocery chains recently put together some very convincing television commercials. The main actor in these ads is a well toned, bright-smiled man with spiked, highlighted hair. He appears to be in his mid-thirties, and also happens to be a doctor. As he strolls through the produce department at one of their stores, he gently grasps or pats fresh fruits and vegetables while he talks about the importance of good eating. You wonder if this is a health seminar or a promo for his next book. Then he concludes the scene by saying this: "Wellness is a choice. Take charge of your health." Next a deep-voiced announcer quickly lets the viewer know of this week's produce specials.

From my viewer's perspective, I like the fact that a grocery store is using a TV MD to encourage the health benefits of eating fresh fruits and veggies. We all know the nutritional gains of just-off-the-vine produce significantly outweigh those of processed fruit snacks. What I don't like about the commercial are the closing words. Is "wellness a choice?" Is it true we can all "take charge of our health?" I guess in a number of contexts this would be true. Healthy eating and exercise do contribute to improved physical health. Yet millions of people are sick due to no failure of their own. Wellness is not a choice for them, nor is chronic illness. Do what they may to try to improve the quality of their lives, they are sentenced to a daily struggle with physical suffering and pain.

I do believe, however, that "soul wellness" is a choice for all people. If the good doctor were to conclude his waltz through the produce department saying, "Do what you can to keep your body strong. And remember. . . keep your soul well in all circumstances," I would support his words 100%. This is the primary theme of this chapter: do everything you can to keep your soul strong and well. The key to soul wellness is healthy thinking. And healthy thinking must be rooted in a sound biblical doctrine of suffering.

What is biblical doctrine? According to Wayne Grudem, "A doctrine is what the whole Bible teaches us today about some particular topic."[12] Sadly, many people (myself included) can be resistant to embrace what the Bible teaches about suffering. We naturally don't want to face the fact that pain and difficulty is a steady theme in the scriptures. Nevertheless for soul wellness we all need to study what God says about pain in the lives of his people. Sound biblical doctrine needs to be rooted deep in our hearts. For when the storms of life come, right thinking will help enable us to persevere for the glory of God.

How I wish I had been more thoroughly grounded in the scriptures when Margaret first became ill. How I regret I did not have a deeper understanding of what the Bible said about suffering in our lives. A real "low-light" of my walk with God in the early years of her illness occurred when I first heard the news she had an autoimmune disease. It took me over two months to tell her the diagnosis. Why? Because I did not have a biblically-based view of suffering. At that point in my life I believed God wanted all his people to be whole in spirit and in body. I believed confessing you were sick meant you were giving in to the affliction, thus letting the devil have his way with you. So, to tell Margaret she had an incurable immune system disease meant I was accepting defeat rather than victory.

Needless to say, embracing an unbiblical doctrine of suffering inevitably leads to a variety of unpleasant consequences. First and foremost, your perspective of who God is consistently fluctuates based on the ups and downs of your circumstances. It looks like this: if Margaret is having a day of good health, God is showing his love and favor. Clearly he is for us. We are experiencing indicators of his pleasure with our lives. If she is being pummeled by a bunch of painful symptoms, the Lord must be displeased. Illness means he's upset

"A Healthy Doctrine of Suffering"

with us. We have somehow fallen out of his blessing. We must search and find the way back to a position of his love and acceptance.

Thinking this way is a shaky rollercoaster ride of the soul. Each day's circumstances become messengers of God's approval (or disapproval) of our lives. Soon to follow can be a host of sinful symptoms, which could include judgmental thoughts, condemnation, anxiety, hopelessness, or a lack of compassion. From my experience, let's just say neglecting what God had to say about suffering made my soul weak and unstable. I was unsure of who he was, and questioned his love and care for us. Pathetically I also quietly wondered if somehow Margaret was to blame for her health woes. What arrogance and lack of compassion I displayed! God wanted my soul grounded in the truth of his word. He didn't want me changing my opinion of him based on the severity of our medical challenges. Poor doctrine does lead to poor living. How I thank God for his mercy to me over the past several years to help me understand more about what the Bible says about suffering.

So, for the next few pages I'd like to highlight some of the key biblical truths about suffering that have transformed our lives. What I am about to write is in no way an in-depth study on the topic of suffering for the Christian. If you'd like to dig deeper, I would highly recommend Timothy Keller's book *Walking with God through Pain and Suffering*, D.A. Carson's book *How Long O Lord*, or Jerry Bridges' book *Trusting God*. These men have said it far better than I ever could, and I am deeply indebted to them for their hard work in completing these excellent books. Their writings have helped me and my family by reinforcing the importance of sound doctrine when it comes to sickness and pain. Here now is a brief list of the key components of a biblical doctrine of suffering. These truths continue to help us in our medical challenges, and I pray they will help you as well.

God is Sovereign

"For his dominion is an everlasting dominion, and his kingdom endures from generation to generation" (Daniel 4:34).

In our lives, this biblical truth has been one of the greatest soul stabilizers: God is sovereign. He is in charge. He reigns over everything. Note these words by theologian J.I. Packer:

The assertion of God's absolute sovereignty in creation, providence, and grace is basic to biblical belief and biblical praise. . . God's dominion is total: he wills as he chooses and carries out all that he wills, and none can stay his hand or thwart his plan.[13]

Think about it. The physical affliction you are facing in your family is no surprise to God. It is part of his eternal plan for you. Despite the severity of our circumstances, it is vital we understand and embrace the fact that God is in control. We can trust him because he allowed the disease or disability, and he knows how it can bring glory to his name.

The biblical doctrine of God's sovereignty is a difficult one to grasp, particularly if you are currently going

"A Healthy Doctrine of Suffering"

through deep waters. It is extremely hard to look at someone you love in agony and believe a loving God has allowed this to happen. It is perplexing to see your body ransacked by disease and embrace the view that a good God reigns over your life. Yet my encouragement to you would be to cling to the truth of the scriptures. The Bible clearly teaches God is the sovereign King of the universe. Nothing can happen to us without his divine permission. So we must trust him no matter how heart-wrenching our circumstances may be.

Here's our great assurance: Margaret's illness is not the result of some random immune system dysfunction. Nor is it an unfortunate act of nature beyond God's control. Her sickness is part of God's mysterious and good plan for our lives. God could have prevented it. He chose not to. Why? We don't know. What we do know is the scriptures clearly teach that the Lord is in control of everything, including sarcoidosis. In a way only God could orchestrate, Margaret's disease is part of his divine will for our lives. So we have hope. If God is in control (and he is), then he knows how all our discomfort can be used for his glory. Thus we can fully trust him with our future. He is sovereign, so we have the confidence he will use her affliction to show us and others his amazing love. (Feel free to jump ahead to chapter seven to read about some of the blessings we have received as a direct result of Margaret's sarcoid.)

The same kind of application applies to everyone who faces a disability or disease. Your child's birth defect, your aging parent's Alzheimer's disease, your sister's spinal cord injury, the crippling arthritis in your feet, your kidney failure, etc, are all under the umbrella of God's control. The pain in your body or the challenges you face as a caregiver are no accident. He loves you, he cares about you, and he is in control. So trust him. Look to him with all your heart. He will guide and strengthen you every step of your medical journey.

All Pain Has a Purpose in God's Plan

"And we know that for those who love God all things work together for good, for those who are called according to his purpose. For those whom he foreknew he also predestined to be conformed to the image of his Son, in order that he might be the firstborn among many brothers" (Romans 8:28-29).

Sometimes I wish Margaret's health struggles were as easy to figure out as one of my assigned algebra homework problems. Despite all the changes I've seen in my twenty-seven-plus years as a professional educator (internet, cell phones, iPods, web-based grading programs, laptops, iPads, and Smartboards, to name a few), the math really hasn't changed. Solving an equation like $4x + 5 = 37$ is done today in virtually the same way it was done when I started my teaching career. (Feel like a high school math flashback? Solve this equation now and then look at my brief explanation in the next sentence.) Do the required inverse operations—subtract five from both sides and then divide by four—and you get the solution $x = 8$. If your answer isn't correct, it's a fairly simple task to find where you went wrong.

Real-life, however, doesn't usually follow the logic of algebra. Particularly in health situations, logic and reason find themselves extinguished by the mystery of

"A Healthy Doctrine of Suffering"

pain and suffering. Why is Margaret ill? What purpose could God possibly have in allowing us years of chronic pain and fatigue? Will we ever be able to look back and see clearly what God had in mind when Margaret was afflicted?

Frankly, I don't anticipate an even partial explanation for the questions I have listed (or a multitude of additional questions I could have listed). Why? Because much of what we experience in this life is a mystery (note the next section of this chapter), and I believe, by faith, God wants us to stand on the reality expressed in Romans 8:28-29. Let's take a closer look at these two verses, with a few key words emphasized by me: "And we know that for those who love God *all* things work together for good, for those who are called according to his purpose. For those whom he foreknew he also predestined *to be conformed to the image of his Son*, in order that he might be the firstborn among many brothers."

Though our finite minds are not capable of understanding what God is trying to accomplish in our lives, the Bible teaches that *all* things do work together to fulfill God's purpose for us. "All" means all. Everything, including chronic disease and disabilities, are part of his good divine plan. Pause and prayerfully let this sink in. God has a purpose for your life. His purpose is good, and is designed to show the world who he is and what he can do. Your pain, your toil as a caregiver, the limitations you face in your body, all of these are part of his good plan. His sovereignty assures us he is in control. His purpose strengthens us to know he will use our pain to show ourselves (and others) his amazing love and power.

As Christians, one significant benefit from our struggles is we are *conformed to the image of his Son.* The Lord desires for us to be more and more like Jesus. Sure, all of us still fail and sin against God. Mercifully, however, God continues to help us to mature in him. He wants us to grow up. Like it or not, suffering is a part of his means to teach us more about our weakness and his strength. Pain in our lives is not a random, meaningless event. Rather, it is allowed by God to deepen our relationship with him, and transform us into the person he wants us to be—more and more like our Savior.

Years ago someone shared this with me: "There is no greater blessing that God can give a man than good health—except for a solid month of illness. For I have seen arrogant, self-sufficient men softened and humbled by physical pain, and come to a deeper realization that God is the true strength of their lives." So too it can be with us. Chronic illness can change our priorities for the better. It can show us we desperately need the Savior when before we could easily forget him. Sickness can show us the love and mercy of God in a profound way.

Though it may sound a bit odd, I thank God for the transforming affect Margaret's health problems have had on my soul. Though I am still very prone to sin, the Lord has taught me much through our years of medical difficulties. I have learned to serve God by loving and caring for her. I have seen God's incredible provision, particularly during those times of intense strain and fear. I have seen much of my own weakness, and the love of God to give me strength during the darkest of times. I love the Savior more, because I have tasted of his daily care and comfort over and over again. Though

I still see my sin and the many areas I need to change, I am grateful for how God continues to use our medical challenges to teach me more about himself. I thank God that pain truly does have a purpose in our lives.

I'd like to conclude this section with these words, penned by Jerry Bridges:

> God has an over-arching purpose for all believers: to conform us to the likeness of His Son, Jesus Christ (Romans 8:29). He also has a specific purpose for each of us that is His unique, tailor-made plan for our individual life (see Ephesians 2:10). And God will fulfill that purpose. As Psalm 138:8 says, "The Lord will fulfill his purpose for me." Because we know He is sovereignly able to orchestrate the events of our lives toward that end, we can trust Him. We can commit to Him not only the ultimate outcome of our lives, but also all the intermediate events and circumstances that will bring us to that outcome.[14]

Get Comfortable with Mystery

"For my thoughts are not your thoughts, neither are your ways my ways, declares the Lord" (Isaiah 55:8).

Numerous times over the years Margaret and I have enjoyed watching episodes of the TV series *Matlock*. Ben Matlock, the star of the show, is a gray-suited, gray-haired Atlanta attorney, with an appetite for tasty hotdogs and a passion for defending people wrongly accused. Played so capably by Andy Griffith (who also looks a lot like Margaret's dad), the show would typically begin with a murder and an arrest, followed by an investigation by Matlock and his legal team. The excitement would reach its peak with courtroom drama, as the aging attorney verbally overwhelms a witness with the blistering heat of a pinpoint cross-examination. At this point the identity of the killer would inevitably be revealed, resulting in the acquittal of the accused. The mystery solved and justice served, each show usually ends with a freeze-frame shot of Matlock casting a wry smile of victorious satisfaction.

I think the only time our hour of *Matlock* has concluded with even a hint of disappointment were those rare shows that ended with the words, "*To Be Continued.*" Neither Margaret nor I planned to spend time watching a murder mystery show only to find out it concludes with no resolution to the mystery. We wanted to see Matlock do his magic. It just didn't seem right to experience all that drama only to be put on hold until the next episode aired.

In our health difficulties we are often met with a similar yet more difficult "*To Be Continued.*" The "whys" of our pain and suffering are not resolved in a timely manner. There are no medical "Matlocks" we can call to get God's explanation as to why we have to carry the burden of an illness or disability. Life is filled with unknowns, particularly when it comes to sickness. Why did Margaret get so sick so early on in our marriage? Why is she sick and not me? Why, despite much prayer and various medical pursuits, is she not completely healed?

Maybe you are wondering similar things. Why is my child ill when all those around me have healthy

"A Healthy Doctrine of Suffering"

children? Why was my husband stricken at such a young age? Why do my children have to see their grandmother slowly deteriorate due to the ravaging affects of cancer?

In the early years of Margaret's illness, I used to always try to figure out what God was trying to show us. Using what I thought were my strong math teacher-related logic skills, I'd search for a clear purpose in her suffering. I wanted to connect the dots between each suffering event, in hopes of somehow finding at least a dimly lit path to explain the why of her disease. Yet the harder I tried to figure it out, the more confused I'd become. Understanding the complexity of God's infinite plan with my finite mind was impossible.

Over the years I've realized it is so much better to live each day trusting in God's sovereign plan. I have accepted the fact there are many things I will never be able to understand. The reality is Margaret's sarcoidosis is a mystery—and I should be OK with that. God's ways are mysterious. His eternal plan is way beyond my ability to comprehend. Frankly, I think it is good to live with things which are mysterious. Why? Because each day I am reminded he is an almighty, infinite, awesome God who is much bigger than I am. Thus he deserves my reverence and my trust during each part of our medical journey. Timothy Keller expresses it this way:

> The point is simple: We are not God. His knowledge and power are infinitely beyond ours... Job 40:2 [ends] with the Lord's question: "Will the one who contends with the Almighty correct him? Let him who accuses God answer him." A seven-year-old cannot question the

mathematical calculations of a world-class physicist. Yet we question how God is running the world. Does that make sense?[15]

How important it is to accept the reality that God's ways, thoughts, and plans are much higher than our own. I would encourage you to think long on the verse at the beginning of this section, which is why I'd like to conclude with it as well. "For my thoughts are not your thoughts, neither are your ways my ways, declares the Lord" (Isaiah 55:6).

Despite the Intensity of the Trial, God's Grace is Always Sufficient

"My grace is sufficient for you, for my power is made perfect in weakness" (2 Corinthians 12:9).

A chronic disease is a medical marathon. Hour upon hour, day after day, the endurance test rages on. Optimism finds little place in a prognosis of increasing pain and disability. Left to ourselves, hope is crushed under the suffocating symptoms of an incurable disease.

Thankfully, however, God has not left us to battle health conditions on our own. He promises to help us through all our ups and downs of physical infirmities. This is the abundant provision given to us by grace through Christ. Who do I mean by grace? A definition I learned years ago used an acronym approach: GRACE = "God's riches at Christ's expense." I would add to this by also saying "it includes all the blessings God has given us through Christ. Those blessings can generally be classified under two categories: privileges and power."[16]

"A Healthy Doctrine of Suffering"

Even though we all deserve punishment for our sins, through Christ, God instead shows his infinite love and goodness toward us. Amazingly, he will (and does) give us all the resources we need to persevere through the battle of physical pain and suffering. We are given the amazing privilege of being his child, forever secure in his eternal love. We are also promised the power to endure times of suffering, all the while given the assurance that every second of pain is under his loving care and control.

This is an incredible reality that brings hope to the soul. *His* grace is sufficient for *you*. We need to realize God's love is so great that there will always be sufficient help in all our times of need. He desires to help us today, tomorrow, and in all the days ahead with his all sufficient grace.

When Margaret's health took a terrible turn for the worse in the fall of 2005, we faced the most difficult time of our lives. It was as if all our greatest fears came at us at once. When she passed out while I was at work, our children were traumatized by having to call 911. Her prognosis was cloaked in mystery, as the doctors tried to figure out what was wrong. Financially we continued to lose ground. The strain was at times unbearable. I would find myself sitting on our back deck, gazing into the sky, begging God to please show us the way out of all these troubles. Sadly, her health continued to deteriorate, and I had no clue what to do next. All I could see was my precious wife struggling to breathe, and I wondered how much more we could take in this medical battle.

How I rejoice and thank God for the biblical doctrine of grace. God promised us (and all of his children) that his grace is, and always will be, sufficient. Miraculously he saw us through, even though things went from bad to worse. Despite the pneumonia that came, the spiraling financial troubles, and the crippling outcome of her prednisone treatment, God gave us the power to endure. The trial didn't destroy us. By his love and mercy, we can now look back and see his wonderful love, care, and provision.

Do your medical circumstances seem more than you can bear? Is the doctor's prognosis putting such a weight on your soul that you feel helpless and hopeless? Focus on the grace of God. He loves you. Through Christ you have been given privileges and the power to endure. As his child, he will never leave you or forsake you. He also will give you the wisdom and strength you need to persevere in a way that honors him.

There really is only one answer to how patients and their families can endure long lasting physical challenges, and still have hope and peace in their lives. It is the all-sufficient grace of God. Thank God for Jesus, and the eternal truth that we do possess "God's riches at Christ's expense."

<u>Physical Healing is in God's Hands</u>

"Is anyone suffering? Let him pray" (James 5:13).

A few years ago I heard a woman on a well-known Christian TV show dogmatically say this: "It is never God's will that you are sick." She followed her declaration by quoting scriptures like Isaiah 53:5b "with his stripes we are healed" and a few other convincing proof texts. She then shared how a relative had been

"A Healthy Doctrine of Suffering"

miraculously healed after a time of diligent prayer and fasting. Her passion and biblical evidence were compelling. But after listening to her for just a few minutes my heart became heavy. I thought of the millions of suffering, sincere, godly people who had yet to see the miracle they'd been praying for. As they toiled and struggled each day in their world of pain and disability, how would her words affect them? If it truly is never God's will for a person to be sick, what kind of soul impact would this position have on folks like me and Margaret? Is it really true God's will for our lives is continual health and physical strength?

As I have studied the scriptures over the years, there is no doubt that God has the power to heal all kinds of physical infirmities. Some of the most amazing examples are in the New Testament. Jesus healed a woman who had a discharge of blood for twelve years (Luke 8:42-44). He gave sight to a man born blind (John 9). In the early church God healed a man who was lame from birth (Acts 3). These passages and others provoke me to realize that at any time God could completely heal Margaret.

Yet the Bible also teaches that God allows his people to be physically afflicted. In these cases there is no account of a miraculous healing. Paul had a thorn in the flesh (2 Corinthians 12:7-8). Timothy had frequent ailments (1 Timothy 5:23). Trophimus was left at Miletus ill (2 Timothy 4:20). There is no biblical record of any of these men being healed. Also, in none of these instances was there any type of rebuke or correction directed towards them. These followers of Christ were not told they had a spiritual deficiency that was the reason for their pain and suffering. No, sickness and physical infirmities were common in the early church just as they are common today. It was (and is) part of the Lord's plan. Also, even a superficial study of church history reveals numerous Christians over the centuries who were blind, afflicted with disease, and faced a host of hardships as they followed the Savior. In our fallen world, medical challenges are a reality, allowed by God to accomplish his will.

My point is that embracing a healthy doctrine of suffering means submitting to God's sovereign plan, even if the plan includes pain and disease. What we continue to learn is the primary issue in our medical battle is living in a way to please the Lord. Sure, we would love to see a reduction in Margaret's pain and continual symptoms. We would gladly welcome a supernatural healing. But what is most important now is we honor God in our sarcoidosis-permeated world. His ways are higher than our ways. We don't understand why she is sick, but we do know he desires to glorify himself through her illness. He gives us grace, purpose, and hope with the disease. So whether a healing comes or not we press on, trusting in his good and mysterious plan for us.

You see, healed or not, the Lord wants us secure in his love. Healed or not, God wants us to live for him. Healed or not, God wants to show the world who he is through our lives. Healed or not, the Lord desires to show his power in our marriage and family. How he demonstrates his love and power is up to him. Today he is manifesting himself by helping us to patiently endure. Someday he may show us his love and power by a miracle of healing. Either way, we know we are loved and cared for by God. His grace is sufficient for each and every one of our needs.

"A Healthy Doctrine of Suffering"

If you have ever wondered about God's will regarding sickness, I would encourage you to pray and study the scriptures. Yes, he can and does at times heal. But if and when he heals is up to him. If you have prayed for years for a healing and none has come, don't lose heart. Don't question his goodness. Don't condemn yourself, and think somehow he is displeased with you. Look freshly at the cross and realize he does love you with an infinite, everlasting love. God will not only see you through, but will use you to show others how amazing he is.

There is so much more that could be said on this topic, but I will again defer to the much more gifted theologians and writers (please read the books I alluded to at the beginning of this chapter). Whether you are currently facing a severe illness or not, now is the time to pray, study, and humbly ask God to help you to understand his doctrine of suffering. Sound biblical doctrine will anchor your soul in your times of medical trouble. It is my prayer your faith will be strong as you remind your soul of the truths we have discussed in this chapter.

Let's hear now from Joni Eareckson Tada, a woman who suffered a serious neck injury as a teenager, and has been a quadriplegic for many years.

> Despite Christ's compassionate death for our sins, God's plan—not plan B or C or D, but his *plan*—calls for all Christians to suffer, sometimes intensely. . . But in God's wisdom and love, every trial in a Christian's life is ordained from eternity past, custom-made for that believer's eternal good, even when it doesn't seem like it. . . God cares most—not about making us

comfortable—but about teaching us to hate our sins, grow up spiritually, and love him.[17]

Discussion Questions

1) What is biblical doctrine?
2) Why is sound biblical doctrine vital to successfully enduring medical trials?
3) Of the key topics mentioned in this chapter, which had the greatest impact on you? Why?

Chapter Four

"God Understands Your World"

> "For we do not have a high priest who is unable to sympathize with our weaknesses, but one who in every respect has been tempted as we are, yet without sin. Let us then with confidence draw near to the throne of grace, that we may receive mercy and find grace to help in time of need" (Hebrews 4:15-16).

Watching movies together is something Margaret and I love to do. Particularly on her really bad health days, enjoying a film in the quiet of our home provides a restful, entertaining activity. Our preferences are normally romantic comedies, or real-life stories that are not too intense. This is why it is a bit surprising that in the last few years we have enjoyed watching the movie *Cast Away*. This film has no romantic comedy elements, nor is it based on any real-life occurrence. Rather, showcasing the acting skills of Tom Hanks, *Cast Away* tells the story of a man (Chuck

Noland) who survived an ocean plane crash only to be stranded for five years on a deserted tropical island.

One of the most unique characters in the movie is named Wilson. What makes Wilson special is he never talks. He never eats. In fact, he isn't even alive. Who is Wilson? He (actually it) is a volleyball, transformed by Noland to have blood-painted facial features and shredded leather hair. Through the long and lonely days and nights on the island, Wilson is Noland's only companion and confidant.

I find it fascinating to observe the significant role Wilson has in Noland's life. When Noland ponders a plan to escape the island, he sounds it off Wilson. At the time when supplies run thin and Noland needs to climb a mountain to retrieve a rope he had made years before, he converses with Wilson, getting the encouragement he needs. In fact, it would seem Noland's mental survival in the film is closely linked to the relationship he has with this now "living" volleyball.

I believe having a chronic illness or disability can place you and your family in your own version of *Cast Away*. Your medical situation has caused you to crash from the normal flow of life. Now you find yourself very much alone on a medical island, with few (if any) who understand what your world is now like. Often you can long for a personal "Wilson" who understands, and can give you the comfort and direction you need. Yet the earnest desire of your soul is for a living companion, not a lifeless, fictitious comrade. No, what you and I need is a real friend who truly understands all the pain we are experiencing.

Do you feel lonely? Is your personal medical version of *Cast Away* bringing you to depths of isolation

"God Understands Your World"

and despair? We can relate. So, I'd like to share with you some key biblical truths that I pray will bring you comfort and strength. To be sure, health challenges come with an almost unavoidable isolation factor, but thank God for the encouragement he provides through Christ. Let's begin with the reality of Jesus' deep understanding of loneliness and rejection.

Christ Understands Loneliness and Rejection

Loneliness is an oppressive companion of chronic disease. Adding to the strain of sickness is the dark cloud of feeling very much alone. Illness and disability frequently put significant relational limitations on both the patient and the caregiver. Health issues will often keep you from social functions and other recreational activities. Plus, many medical conditions simply don't travel well. It can take hours for the patient to shower and get ready to leave the house, only to then arrive at the desired destination fatigued and in pain. Often the patient prefers to stay at home, where a comfortable bed and medical supplies are near. And, as the patient stays home, typically so does the caregiver.

For us, Margaret is now able to get out of the house around once or twice a month. With her mobility issues, she usually requires about two hours to get ready to leave. While she is getting ready I get everything in place to make the journey from our front door to our car as safe as possible. This involves getting her wheelchair positioned in the hallway, setting up a portable ramp off our front threshold, and making sure her oxygen tank is in the car. I help her get dressed, carefully drive her in her wheelchair to our driveway, and then assist her as she transitions from the wheelchair to passenger side seat of our car. Despite all the effort involved, most of these "escapes" from our home are for medical appointments.

Many times over the years we have had to miss worship services, picnics, birthday parties, and a host of other fun social events. Our missing of these get-to-gethers has prevented opportunities for us to get to know people, and for people to get to know us. With the unpredictability of Margaret's disease, usually we don't know until just a few hours before an event whether or not we will be able to attend. Our entire social calendar is related to (and, it seems, is ruled by) sarcoidosis.

Another facet of chronic disease isolation is it is hard to find people who can relate personally to your world. Most everyone knows what it is like to get sick, let the illness run its course, and then feel better. The chronic illness world, however, is another zone all together. It is difficult for most folks to relate to a sickness or family health condition that is *always* there. Your affliction *never* takes a vacation. Your family is seldom, if ever, given a moment of caregiver down time. The pain stays and often progresses. The toil of lovingly providing for the afflicted loved one is a huge part of each and every day. So, even the most caring of people usually can't honestly tell you they know how you feel. They really don't understand your life of challenge, because they haven't lived it like you have.

What can also be disappointing is when people draw conclusions about your disease. These subtle (or not so subtle) conclusions can cut to the heart, and add rejection to the mix of your medical difficulties.

"God Understands Your World"

As I mentioned earlier, when Margaret first became ill, we heard everything from "It's all in your head," to "You are ill because you drank diet cola," to "There must be some unconfessed sin in your life." Inside our apartment we were dealing with the strain of her disease. Outside of our apartment we had to deal with the social withdrawal of those who felt Margaret was somehow to blame for her illness.

Feelings of rejection can also come simply from the famine of beneficial social interaction. People may not say they don't want to spend time with you, but the omission of being included leaves a sting of desertion. Few calls, few invites, coupled with little to no conversations with others outside your family can tempt you to think the worst of people.

I remember a Sunday a number of years ago when the severity of Margaret's symptoms required us to miss the morning worship service at our church. Later that day, as the clock approached dinner time, I thought to myself, "Boy, the phone hasn't rung in awhile. Why hasn't anyone called us today? I wonder. . . Is there is a single person who really cares about us?"

Then it was as if I slowly allowed myself to be transformed into a think-a-like of Eeyore from *Winnie the Pooh*. Remember Eeyore? He is the ever despondent, never optimistic donkey with the pinned-on tail. It looked like this: I moped around the house, feeling gloomy, wondering if anyone really loved us. Then I thought, "O well, another day of hardship. Woe is me. No one has time for me. I might as well just sit here and see what other lonely hardships come our way."

Regretfully, my mind didn't stop there. Next I focused on a number of self-serving questions: "Why do people seldom ask how we are doing? Don't they realize we haven't been to church in two weeks? Don't they understand the magnitude of our suffering? Why don't we see more Christian love pointed in our direction?"

My attitude was a sinful blend of a self-centered, self-serving, loneliness and rejection. We were on our isolated medical island, with no rescue "planes" in sight, and no visible attempts of compassionate outreach. I wondered if the folks we knew felt like we were too much of a bother, you know, the high maintenance family. Were we being subtly deserted? Did no one think we were really worth their time?

Thankfully God forgave me that day and for the numerous times since then that I have morphed into the Eeyore mind-set. You see, if our hope and joy is based on what people are doing for us, we will never be satisfied. What I have seen is people will do what they can to bring the comfort of God to you in your affliction. They will do and say the most encouraging things they can think of to help. These acts of kindness and care are precious, and are a blessing from God.

I have often sinned against God because I wanted people (hey, expected people), to be my supernatural "Wilsons." I put an unrealistic expectation on folks to intimately and expertly be able to give me all the help I felt I deserved. The reality is that *only* God completely understands all the aspects of your chronic disease world. Particularly in the area of loneliness and rejection, our great Savior knows intimately what you are facing.

A huge comfort to me, particularly when I feel alone, is the knowledge that Jesus knows loneliness. He, more than anyone else, can empathize with the

"God Understands Your World"

darkness and silent suffering that rejection and isolation can bring. Let's look at a few scriptural highlights of how we can know of his deep love and understanding for those who feel rejected, isolated and forgotten.

From the early days of his ministry, Jesus knew the sting of rejection and isolation. Even a casual reading of the Gospel of John reveals a number of events where the Lord is being misunderstood, hated, and rejected. Here are just a few:

•After healing a man at a pool on the Sabbath, the Jews wanted to kill him (John 5:18).

•After he taught about being the "bread of life," the Jews grumbled about him (John 6:41-42).

•In response to his teaching, many of his followers "turned back and no longer walked with him" (John 6:66).

•Others accused him of having a demon (John 7:20).

Yes, our loving Savior fully knows what it is like to be with few friends. He completely empathizes with rejection and being left alone.

Also, in the events before and during his crucifixion, the Lord experienced the desertion of many of those who were closest to him. Note these sad events:

•One of the twelve, Judas Iscariot, betrayed him with a kiss (Luke 22:47).

Always Sick, Always Loved

• The nation that he had lived among and ministered to demanded he be crucified (Luke 23:20-23).

• Even the disciple Peter, when asked about knowing Jesus, denied him (Luke 22:56-60).

• Of all his disciples, it appears only John was actually present at the crucifixion (John 19:25-26).

In his time of greatest suffering, few supporters were found near him.

Then, in the ultimate act of redeeming love, Christ experienced, for the first time in his eternal existence, the rejection of God the Father. When he became sin for us, in that agonizing moment on the cross, "Jesus cried with a loud voice, Eloi, Eloi, lema sabachthani?, which means, My God, my God, why have you forsaken me?" (Mark 15:34) Note the explanation of his cry by John Stott:

No theology is genuinely Christian which does not arise from and focus on the cross. In particular, by 'the cross'. . . means more than anything else the cry of dereliction. It shows. . . that Jesus was not only rejected by the Jews as a blasphemer and executed by the Romans as a rebel, but actually condemned and abandoned by his Father. . . What, then, do we understand of God when we see the crucified Jesus and hear his derelict cry? We certainly see his willingness in love to identify with human rejects.[18]

"God Understands Your World"

There can be no doubt that Jesus understands loneliness and all that relates to it. He experienced the penalty for our sins. He experienced the desertion of most of those closest to him. He saw people question his motives, his ministry, and his integrity. Surely he understands, when as a chronically ill person, you taste of the depths of loneliness and isolation. He knows what it is like to be cut off from those you want to be with, facing the challenges of life seemingly alone.

Getting back to the *Cast Away* illustration, I believe God wants us first and foremost to realize the real "Wilson" on our medical island is him. He wants us to grow in our understanding that he is our true refuge when the crash of chronic disease shakes our world. Look again at the scripture written at the beginning of this chapter: "For we do not have a high priest who is unable to sympathize with our weaknesses, but one who in every respect has been tempted like as we are, yet without sin. Let us then with confidence draw near to the throne of grace, that we may receive mercy, and find grace to help in time of need" (Hebrews 4:15-16).

The application of these verses is profound, particularly for those who are suffering. First, Jesus is not a Savior "who is unable to sympathize with our weaknesses." In other words, he understands what we are going through. How I need to let this truth sink in each and every day. He understands, not partially, but completely. He chose to enter our world and suffer. He feels our pain. He knows our struggle. He has tasted of isolation and rejection. He can fully relate to our chronic illness world. If I want to come to someone who truly, really understands, I must come to Jesus. He knows all about affliction. He suffered more than anyone who has ever walked this earth. He is our compassionate, loving Lord.

Secondly, in light of his understanding of pain and weakness, he tells me to pray to him with confidence. God wants us to come to him. He desires for us to draw near and find the help we need. This is an amazing truth: the living God desires for us to come near to him, and he also wants to give us all the help we need to endure our medical challenges. Feeling overwhelmed and hopeless? Are you under the dark cloud of loneliness? Are you exhausted physically and emotionally? Come to the living Savior. He is our true refuge. He will faithfully take care of you and your family.

Praise God, this has been our testimony. Sure, we have made mistakes along the way. Just pausing now, however, and thinking of how the Lord has wonderfully cared for us over these past twenty-five-plus years is truly phenomenal. When I have cried out to him during my times of exhaustion, he has renewed my strength. When we have longed for wisdom, he has given it to us. When we have needed various kinds of help, God has always been there, giving us the grace we needed. How we thank God for his compassion for us, and his faithful daily care.

It is this theme of drawing near to God that fuels the remainder of this chapter. Since he wants us to confidently draw near to him, I thought I'd conclude this section of the book by looking at some of my top reasons, particularly during seasons of suffering, we should consistently talk to the Savior. (And, if you are not currently going through some difficult times, these are still good reasons to pray as well.)

"God Understands Your World"

The Need for a Biblical Perspective

"For it is God who works in you, both to will and to work for his good pleasure" (Philippians 2:13).

Several months ago I had a unique experience during a Sunday morning worship service. As our church's congregation was singing, I kept hearing the steady pulse of an oxygen concentrator. If you have never heard an O_2 concentrator in action, it has a consistent mechanical beat followed by a hissing sound. The repeated beat-hiss, beat-hiss, beat-hiss, alerted me that someone nearby was using oxygen. Since Margaret has been using oxygen for years now, I was super-sensitized to the sound. I knew someone sitting fairly close to me must have a pretty serious health challenge.

As the music ended and we were given a short time to visit with those around us, I quickly scanned the folks near me to see who was using the concentrator. In a few moments I spotted a man in his mid-forties, very thin and ashen-faced, with the opaque tubing of his cannula securely fixed into his nose. Standing close by his side was his wife, smiling as she met a few people sitting next to them. I knew after the service this was a couple I had to meet.

When our pastor's message ended about forty-five minutes later, I worked my way a few rows back and introduced myself to them. Though I don't remember their names, what I do recall is the obvious peace and joy in their lives. His wife, a blond-haired woman with a strong German accent, told me how her husband had been diagnosed with a rare lung disease. From what I could discern his prognosis wasn't very good. He spoke just a few words to me, but his contagious smile and hopeful outlook on life inspired my heart. As we concluded our brief conversation, I simply stated, "Wow, the joy I see in your lives, it so encourages me. Thank you for your great testimony." Then his wife succinctly replied, "Well, we decided a number of years ago that this would make us better, not bitter."

The perspective this couple had embraced is one I believe the Lord wants all to embrace who are facing difficult medical trials. God is in control. He has allowed our affliction. He will use our pain to show others who he is. So, by his strength we will not be angry and bitter. We will not think God is unfair. Rather, we will take the biblical perspective that God will use this trouble to make us grow. We will by faith believe that our outcome will be better. Better, not because we are guaranteed a happy ending, but better because we will know Jesus in a deeper way. Such an attitude, one that trusts God and has a Bible-based faith perspective, can only come from God. To experience this kind of biblical perspective, you and I must spend time often with the Lord in prayer.

As I described in chapter one, our current medical reality is a blend of increasing pain, disability, and potentially life-threatening symptoms. There is no happy ending waiting for us on our medical horizon. Everyday Margaret is in pain. Her body continues to physically erode. Age is accelerating the progression of her sarcoidosis. As the days pass, the disabling effects of her illness are getting worse—and there is nothing we can do to stop it.

When I see her suffering, there is always an internal battle going on inside of me. It is the war of

"God Understands Your World"

perspective. Her medical condition creates a visual message, tempting me to wonder if God really loves us. So as my day begins, and I taste my first few sips of coffee, I start by asking the Lord to give me his perspective. I need his help to see our troubles through the lens of biblical truth.

So, by his grace I open my Bible and read verses of his faithfulness to us. I remind my soul of his doctrine of suffering. I read devotional books out loud, so both Margaret and I can be encouraged in who God is. I ask him to enable me to look beyond our challenges and to see Christ's love through the gospel. I thank him for the promise of his care today. By his strength, I want her illness to make us more like Jesus. I pray I will not grumble and complain, but rather I will be a thankful person, rejoicing in God's amazing love for us.

It is so imperative, when an illness or disability comes, that we are not shaken in our conviction of who God is. We need to think biblically. Yes, when Margaret is extremely ill, the suffering I see tempts me to mentally question what the Bible teaches about God. I can wonder, "Does God *really* love us? Sure, Jesus died on the cross and rose again, but look at the agony she is going through. Our doctors give us little hope, I am being pressed into triple duty, and I just don't see God in our circumstances. Can I really believe all the Bible teaches about the Lord and how he relates to our pain?"

Thankfully, I am learning that through prayer the Lord can remind me of the truths of the gospel. I can be confident and unwavering in the reality of who God is. His love at Calvary proves he is always with us. He loved us when we were lost and dead in our sins. We are eternally in his family, forever secure in his love. No suffering in this life can ever separate us from the love of Christ, nor is suffering a sign that his attitude toward us has changed.

So, my encouragement to you would be to pray daily for a biblical perspective. Review over and over again the truths I've shared in chapters two and three. Is your loved one stricken with a serious illness? Is the daily grind of being a caregiver wearing you down? Are you seriously wondering if God still cares about you and your family? Ask God to renew your outlook through the truths of his word. Prayerfully think long about the gospel, and the sovereignty of God. Fix your eyes on the Savior, and taste the peace, joy, and hope only he can give. Determine in the depths of your heart to trust God to make you "better, not bitter."

I'd like to conclude this section with a gospel-encouragement from C.J. Mahaney:

> The gospel should be at the center of your prayer life... There's nothing complicated about this. To pray the gospel, simply begin by thanking God for the blessing of eternal life, purchased through the death of His Son. Acknowledge that Christ's work on the cross is what makes your very prayer possible. . . We come by the cross, we have the right to ask boldly because of the cross. The gospel should be woven in throughout our praise, our petition, and our intercession.[19]

"God Understands Your World"

The Need for Wisdom

"If any of you lacks wisdom, let him ask of God, who gives generously to all without reproach, and it will be given him" (James 1:5).

Yogi Berra, the legendary Yankee catcher, once was quoted as saying, "You've got to be very careful if you don't know where you are going because you might not get there."[20] In Yogi's special, humorous way, he is telling us we need direction in our lives. It is vital we know where we are going, lest we find "we might not get there."

How do we figure out where we are supposed to go in our medical journey? In the information age in which we live, just a few clicks on a mouse will give us literally hundreds of pages of information. Do an internet search on your family's chronic health condition, and you'll find virtually anything (and everything) about the disease: typical symptoms, atypical symptoms, prognosis, traditional treatments, holistic treatments, stories of healing, horrific tales of death, medication options, medications to avoid, helpful diets, treatment centers, and just about anything else medically-related you'd like to know. So what do you do with all this medical information? My encouragement—ask God for wisdom.

One of my biggest regrets in the early years of Margaret's affliction is that I seldom asked God for his direction. Her doctors would prescribe a regimen of treatment, and I thought, since they were the medical professionals, they must be right. I was just a lowly math teacher. They had medical degrees and years of experience treating diseases. Who was I to question

Always Sick, Always Loved

their judgment, let alone ask God to show me if their plan was the best plan for her treatment?

What I have learned, however, is how vital it is to ask God for wisdom. I believe his will is that I talk to him often about Margaret's medical care. He wants to guide us, but I won't sense his leading if I am not patiently asking him to direct our steps. Particularly over the past few years, there have been specific times when we have told her physicians we didn't agree with a change in her treatment plan. I believe the Lord has lovingly warned us not to try new, more experimental medications. He has also steered us to different physicians who are more knowledgeable and compassionate about sarcoidosis. I thank God that he encourages us to come to him with all our medical questions and concerns. He desires to give us wisdom.

I would still passionately encourage all patients and caregivers to do their medical homework. Use all the resources you can to understand what medically is going on. Search the internet—read books—talk to people who understand the affliction you are facing. Be as knowledgeable as you possibly can. Still, make praying to God your highest priority. Know the disease, but seek to know him even more, for he is the one who will use what you have learned to direct your medical decisions.

When we were first told Margaret had sarcoidosis, in our desperation we prayed long and hard. The pain in her body paralleled the ache we felt in our souls. We didn't understand what our future would look like with this incurable disease, and we tried to talk to the Lord about all our fears. Yet when we weren't praying, we were often on our computer, finding out everything we could about sarcoidosis. In addition, we were calling

"God Understands Your World"

family members who had some knowledge of the disease, getting not only their prayer support, but also their medical insight. I found out that a secretary at my school had been treated for sarcoid years before. She became a key provider of information that helped us understand what to expect as Margaret's steroid treatment began. Clearly the information we gathered helped us make wiser medical decisions.

I think a good illustration about the balance of doing your own research and seeking God would be similar to how I would counsel a Christian student to prepare for a test in one of my classes. If you were in my block four geometry class (now there's a dream for you to ponder. . . four to five hours of math instruction per week, daily assignments, weak math humor) I'd tell you the following: "The key to acing my exams is to study. Go over the test review worksheet at least two to three times. Look over your homework assignments. Create additional practice problems to master the concepts. Pray as well, but make sure you have worked hard to know the material." The reality is, few students I have had over the years, as much as they may have prayed, have done well without also doing the hard work of preparation.

Do you need God's wisdom for yourself or a loved one? Humbly ask God what to do, then roll up your sleeves and do your medical homework. Let him broaden your medical understanding and wisdom. God desires to show us the way we should go. How grateful I am that over the years he has faithfully given us wisdom, and I pray we will continue to not depend on our own ideas, but rather keep him first in all our medical choices.

The Need for Peace

"Do not be anxious about anything, but in everything by prayer and supplication with thanksgiving let your requests be made known to God. And the peace of God, which surpasses all understanding, will guard your hearts and minds in Christ Jesus. Finally brothers, whatever is true, whatever is honorable, whatever is just, whatever is pure, whatever is lovely, whatever is commendable, if there is any excellence, if there is anything worthy of praise, think about these things. What you have learned and received and heard and seen in me—practice these things, and the God of peace will be with you" (Philippians 4:6-9).

Disease and disability have a close colleague called anxiety. With frightening prognoses and endless unknowns, patients and caregivers can face serious struggles with overwhelming worry. For me, anxiety is like a predator waiting for an opportunity. When I lose focus and begin to look at our challenges outside the truth of God's loving care, worrisome thoughts are soon to follow.

My biggest anxiety overload came after Margaret's sarcoidosis' diagnosis in the fall of 2005. After spending hours camped in front of my computer researching her illness, my brain began to spin an array of not-so-pleasant scary scenarios. It was a cranial, reality-based medical drama, characterized by ever-increasing symptoms and family pressures. Visualizing her steady physical decline, picturing a daily grind of caregiving duties, and then seeing it all culminating in Margaret's death, didn't inspire me to faith and hope. All I could see was our family on the path of devastation, our finances spiraling downward, and me being left alone to raise our children. Yes, in my den of sarcoid-inspired images I was overwhelmed with what I feared the future held for us.

I was living the anxiety-tainted reality expressed by Linda Dillow:

> Worry is like a rocking chair; it will give you something to do but it won't get you anywhere... All our fret and worry are caused by calculating without God... When we worry, we're saying, "God can't." If we are walking in anxiety, we're not walking in faith. We want to be [people] of faith, yet often worry becomes our middle name. We know the agony of its clutches. We're familiar with the small trickle of fear that meanders through our minds until it cuts a channel into which all other thoughts are drained. We must conquer this "God can't" disease.[21]

The truth is that many of my scary mental images then (and now) may in fact occur. Diseases do typically progress, leaving in their wake added symptoms and additional hardship. When fear begins to dominate my thoughts, however, I have learned that I must come to the Lord. Quickly I need to pray, and remind myself of who he is. God is living and reigning over our lives. There is no "fear factor" with him. His desire is to give us the miraculous assurance that he is in control, and will be with us every step of the medical journey. It is the peace of God that he wants us to experience, no matter how stressful our circumstances may be.

A wonderful benefit of a personal, saving relationship with Christ is peace. As believers, we have a spiritual buffet of promises, some of which I have already discussed. Amazingly and supernaturally, another promise God has for his child is his peace. Even in the severest storms of medical uncertainty, our souls can be at rest, peaceful in the assurance of God's never-ending love, care, and sovereignty.

Note these inspiring comments on Philippians 4:6-9 by J.A. Motyer:

> The first promise is that our lives will be touched with a mark of the supernatural, something that *passes all understanding* (verse 7). The meaning here is not of something mysterious and incomprehensible in its own right, but of something men cannot explain or explain away; something which runs beyond the range of human comprehension. . . The second promise is that God's peace will guard us and God himself will be our companion: *the peace of God. . . will keep. . . the God of peace will be with you.* This is the picture of a besieged citadel. It is the castle of the mind of a Christian. . . Inside the citadel, hearts and thoughts alike are kept in quietness, for their Companion is the King himself, *the God of peace* who is with them.[22]

Are you stressing over various aspects of your medical situation? Is the prognosis of you or your loved one's disease crushing you with prison-like fear? Here's

"God Understands Your World"

God's desire for you: "*Do not be anxious about anything.*" Yet you may wonder, how is it possible? Looking at my sick child, my disabled parent, seeing the toll my health condition is having on our family, how can I possibly not be anxious?

Well, God shows us the way to freedom from anxiety. He tells us "*In everything, by prayer and supplication with thanksgiving, let your requests be made known to God.*" Simply stated, the Lord wants us to talk to him about everything that troubles us. Worried about the projected course of a disease? Discuss it with the Lord. Fearful about upcoming medical bills? Take time to talk it over with the living God. Wondering how you will be able to keep caring for your disabled loved one? Give the concern to the Lord. Freshly put your hope and trust in him, and ask him to give you the experience of his supernatural peace.

This is his amazing promise: "*And the peace of God, which surpasses all understanding, will guard your hearts and minds in Christ Jesus.*" God can give you a peace that is beyond human understanding. It is a heaven-sent peace, a fruit of his powerful Holy Spirit. As we pray, talking over all our troubles with him, he will comfort and strengthen us with his incredible peace.

God's peace is something I long to experience in an ever-growing, deeper way. Still at times I can live like a worrisome child, who doesn't trust his Father to provide for him. How I pray that with increasing measure I will rest in his love and care. With more medical tests on our horizon, I am grateful for the provision of God's peace. I know that as I talk to the Lord about Margaret's test results and whatever additional medical difficulties we may face, he can (and will) empower us with peace. By his grace we can anticipate a real calmness of the soul no matter what the future holds.

So, my encouragement would be, when you are anxious, pray. Enter into prayer thanking God for all he has done for you. Thank him for your salvation, and Jesus' redemptive work on the cross. Praise him for his word, and all the truths that affirm his divine care. Then openly and honestly present your needs to God. Talk to him about everything. Tell him about your fears. Tell him about all the confusion you feel. Give to him all your burdens, from the lightest to the weightiest. Then, through his loving provision, experience his precious peace.

In conclusion, let's not forget the incredible reality that the living God understands our struggles. If you are sacrificing your time and energy to care for a disabled loved one, God knows what your day looks like. He completely knows your hidden difficulties and fears. When you are up in the night, he knows your fatigue and despair. When you feel all alone, he knows what you are going through. When you don't understand how you will pay the medical bill you have just read, he wants to intimately encourage you and show you his way of provision. Yes, God truly understands your medical world, and desires to show you his amazing strength, love, and peace each and every step of the way. Once again, let's dwell on the words of Joni Eareckson Tada:

> I recall years ago in the hospital when Jesus came through as my friend. There were times when He was my one and only comfort during dark lonely

"God Understands Your World"

nights after visiting hours. . . Talking with Jesus strengthened my confidence in Him, a friend who would ultimately see me through months of suicidal depression at the prospect of permanent paralysis. He was the one who lent a sympathetic ear, His eye contact never faltering.[23]

By God's love and mercy, may we be praying patients and caregivers. Let's come to him confidently in prayer with grateful hearts. Let's pray that we will be able to say with the Psalmist, "I sought the Lord, and he answered me and delivered me from all my fears" (Psalm 34:4).

Discussion Questions

1) How do you know Christ understands loneliness and rejection?
2) When was the last time, in an open and honest way, you talked to the Lord about the trials you are facing? What was that experience like for you?
3) Why is it important to consistently pray?

Chapter Five

"Learning Contentment"

"Not that I am speaking of being in need, for I have learned in whatever situation I am to be content. I know how to be brought low, and I know how to abound. In any and every circumstance, I have learned the secret of facing plenty and hunger, abundance and need. I can do all things through him who strengthens me" (Philippians 4:11-13).

A few years ago I spent a pleasant Saturday afternoon watching my daughter Liz compete in a volleyball tournament. The hour and fifteen minute drive to Greeley, Colorado, gave me some quality time with her, as we discussed everything from school to her upcoming track season. The bright sunshine and forty degree temperature outside made the drive a peaceful one, as the sometime unpredictable Colorado weather stayed calm. Once we arrived in Greeley, however, stillness and peaceful conversation were displaced by the

"Learning Contentment"

sound of almost forty teams competing for the tournament championship. If you have never been in a building hosting eight simultaneous volleyball matches, it is an unforgettable experience. The blend of intense competition, enthusiastic cheering, and teens diving for crucial "digs," made for a memorable afternoon.

During a break between matches, one of the parents of Liz's teammates struck up a conversation with me. As we talked about work, our families, and our life's challenges, he told me how much he hated it when his life wasn't full of positive things. As he put it, "When my life is only half full, I want it at least 95% full—and I will do whatever I can to get it full again. I simply won't sit back and accept the fact that my life has troubles that make it seem half empty—or worse."

Though I appreciated his determined zeal to not accept any negative circumstances in his life, the reality is that troubles are inescapable. As passionate as we may be to change or rid ourselves of difficulty, often there really is no path of escape. This is how the chronic illness world operates. It is an existence of often irreversible, incurable affliction. As much as we want our lives to be filled with positive, clearly beneficial things, there is no exit out of our pain and challenges. Like it or not, we have entered into the struggle of learning contentment.

I find as I write these sentences, my mind drifts to the Pixar movie *A Bug's Life*. Yes, I acknowledge it is a bit odd (or more than a bit odd) that a fifty-five-year-old man would find his mind filling with images of animated insects joining together to ward off evil grasshoppers, particularly as I discuss as important a topic as contentment. Yet a line in the movie seems applicable here—and it is spoken by a large annoyed horse fly.

The scene I am thinking of is early in the movie, and involves a sparsely attended circus performance. The audience, a collage of flies and other assorted insects, are quickly losing interest in the low quality acts of the circus bugs. In the sea of boos and agitated insect observers, a large fly (who looks like he could have been a steroid abuser) states, "I've got twenty-four hours to live, and I ain't gonna waste it here."

Frankly, I find the fly's feelings and attitude very relevant to the life of chronic disease. He figured his time on this planet was short, and it shouldn't be wasted stuck in some deplorable scenario. In many ways people facing chronic illness can fall into the same line of thinking. Focusing on their circumstances and all the challenges that come with them, it is all too easy to question the why of it all. We are given one short span of time on the earth. Shouldn't that time be filled with an abundance of happy memories, with only an occasional season of difficulty? If you are like me, your thoughts, (in *A Bug's Life's* fashion) can whine, "I've only got around seventy years to live, and why do most of them have to be confined to the world of chronic disease?"

Recently, Margaret described her life with sarcoidosis as "being imprisoned in my own body." Her daily routine of navigating our home with a walker, being on oxygen, and struggling to do even the simplest of tasks is a jail of inflamed flesh and bone. It is an incarceration with a life sentence—no cure, no relief, no opportunity to get out on parole. People on the "outside" are waking up and are able to do whatever they want to. Folks in the Alcatraz of chronic disease usually face

"Learning Contentment"

years of hard labor, left to wonder why God has left them in their cell of pain and suffering.

It is not too surprising, then, when chronic sufferers are tempted to take matters into their own hands. It is hard to trust God and have a positive outlook on the future when medically all is bleak. When a patient realizes his health condition is incurable, and his future is likely to be filled with years of pain, hopelessness can easily sink in. The patient may choose to abuse his medications to dull the pain. He may ponder or attempt suicide to end his bondage of suffering.

For the caregiver, he may follow a strategy of gradual withdrawal; progressively filling his life with other activities to get relief and escape from his medical labor. At its worst, I have seen some folks, facing the weight of providing long-term care for a loved one, choose a heart-tearing permanent retreat. With destroying words like, "I didn't sign up for *this*," he walks away, turning his back on responsibility in favor of an easier life. This rejection of medical circumstances leaves in its wake the catastrophe of a shattered family—and a patient emotionally ripped to shreds.

Yes, left to ourselves, it is impossible to find contentment in the sickness world. Bitterness, anger, and discontentment are the attitudes that naturally come out of our hearts. Dogged human determination will eventually run out of steam. The days, months, and years of disability and pain are just too long to endure successfully on our own.

Thank God, Jesus promises to be with us every step of the way. Nothing can separate us from his love and care. He assures us that he will provide our every need. He gives us hope that our family will not be destroyed by the medical hardships, but will actually be strengthened by his divine love and comfort. Only Christ, and the amazing grace of God, can bring peace, contentment, and the perseverance necessary to endure the challenges of chronic disease. His desire is not that you just survive your medical trials. He wants you, as a Christian, to actually experience peace, joy, and contentment while the suffering continues. Impossible you say? Yes, it is impossible if all we had to rely on were human resources. Yet with the help of God it can be our reality.

I realize as you read this you may be feeling plagued by discontentment. You might be like the middle-aged woman the kids and I saw a few years ago. We first noticed her as she was painstakingly making the trek across the parking lot at our local department store. With an aluminum walker in front of her, she stiffly swung her legs to move herself just a foot or so at a time. It took her a number of minutes to navigate the twenty yards from her car to the entrance of the store. As she came closer to us, I could see the trembling of her hands, and the strained look in her eyes. Despite her severe physical limitations, what was most visible to me was her anger and frustration. As we held the store doors open for her, she gruffly said to me, "Isn't this pathetic. A woman my age and I can't even get through a door." As she went past us, I took a moment and silently prayed for her. For without knowing the love of Christ, Margaret and I would be just like her. . . or worse. What she needed more than physical relief was a transformation of her heart. She needed to understand the personal love of Jesus. She needed the grace

"Learning Contentment"

of God to learn and experience the contentment that only he can give.

How about you? Can you relate to what this woman was experiencing? Do you find yourself often frustrated and discontent? Do you long for peace, rest, and contentment in your soul? I pray as you continue to read this chapter that the Lord will touch your heart. May he help you to experience the contentment that only Christ can give.

What does it mean to be content? According to John MacArthur, it means "to be satisfied."[24] In other words, a life of contentment means you find satisfaction no matter what your circumstances. It is not about whether you perceive your personal glass as half full or half empty. It is not about whether your medical prognosis is favorable or not. It is realizing in the depths of your soul an inner peace and satisfaction with your lot in life. Whether circumstances are easy or hard, it is an inner gratefulness to God, and an assurance that he loves you, and will faithfully care for you every step of the way.

So, here lies the pinnacle question of this section. Can a person *really* learn to be content (i.e. satisfied with his or her life) when each day is consumed with dealing with a chronic health issue? With God's help, the answer is amazingly, *Yes*! Please read on, for I think you will be encouraged as we look at some key aspects of contentment.

Learning Contentment Through Our Relationship with God

I believe at the heart of contentment has to be an inner satisfaction and dependence on God himself. Despite all our best intentions, there simply is no way any of us can determine we are going to be content, particularly when we are dealing with continual health-related challenges. Human fortitude cannot make someone satisfied during times of adversity. A person cannot "work up" contentment. Learning contentment can only come with the help of God.

If you are like me, it is all too easy to try to use human resources to create a state of contentment. A common trap that leads to "pseudo-contentment" is comparing our suffering to the suffering of others. I aim to feel better about our circumstances by looking at what people worse off than us are dealing with. For example, I hear a co-worker has breast cancer, which will require her to have surgery and chemotherapy. So, I thank God Margaret's sarcoidosis doesn't require such an aggressive treatment regimen. I find out a neighbor is losing his home through foreclosure; I am grateful because I am still able to make our house payment, despite ongoing medical costs.

As I continue to focus on other's situations that are more severe than our own, somehow I feel a bit better about things. I create a nuance of satisfaction, since things could be much more difficult. This is *not* the contentment God desires to work in my life. It is not contentment at all, but rather a twisted feel-good approach based on the severity of the sufferings of others. What I really need is God-given change in my heart. I need for the Lord to teach me true, soul contentment.

I am very grateful that the Apostle Paul said he had *"learned* in whatever situation I am to be content" (Philippians 4:11b). The implication here is that contentment is something we grow in. The path of contentment is a process. Step by step, day by day, the Lord desires to teach us how to be content, no matter what the circumstances of our lives.

As a high school math teacher, each unit I teach is a sequential, planned process of learning. In the linear equation unit, for example (I trust as I inject another math illustration, you won't feel too sedated), I begin with some key foundational number skills which involve integer operations. Then I proceed after integer operations with the concept of combining variable expressions. Next, variable expressions are used to solve basic algebraic equations. Then the complexity of equations gradually increases, with variables on both sides of the equal sign being the key equation threshold for most freshman algebra students. The curriculum is logical, with a specific timeline, and has a clearly defined learning goal. If I do my job, and the students do theirs, then mathematical learning is demonstrated on the unit assessment, and all is well in my math world.

In the realm of contentment, there is also a specific, sequential learning process orchestrated by God. First and foremost, a person must have a solid foundation in their soul. It must be a foundation of truth, based on a personal, saving relationship with Jesus Christ.

So, I once again must point to the gospel of Christ. Jesus is the only one who can bring a true transformation of the soul. At the instant of salvation his life-changing work begins, and "He who began a good work in you will bring it to completion at the day of Jesus Christ" (Philippians 1:6). When the foundation of Christ is in your soul, the God-directed process of learning contentment has begun. Step by step, his desire is to teach you how to be content, no matter what your current circumstances may be. For sure, learning contentment can be a painful and challenging process. It is a state of the soul that can only come from the fruit that comes from God. Yet despite our sinful tendencies it is possible. It is possible because of what Christ has done in us. As the Apostle exclaims, "I can do all things through him who strengthens me" (Philippians 4:13). Ponder these words written by David Powlison:

> You need the invasion of the Redeemer, the hand of the Shepherd. You need great help, the way a drowning man needs great help from outside himself to rescue him. Only one thing is strong enough to overpower and slay unruly cravings and a stormy life: what God promises to do in and through Jesus Christ. It is by precious and very great promises that we escape the corruption that is in the world by lust (2 Peter 1:4). From God's side, we escape ourselves by being loved by Jesus Christ through the powerful presence of the Holy Spirit Himself. From our side, we escape ourselves by learning a lifestyle of intelligent repentance, genuine faith, and specific obedience.[25]

In my life, if I am going to be content in God I must look beyond my circumstances. If my satisfaction is

"Learning Contentment"

based on what I see, contentment in the Lord is impossible. Margaret's pain and ongoing symptoms scream to my soul that I have a right to complain and be bitter at God. Why should I be thankful and content in the Lord when my life is filled with an ongoing medical trial with a pessimistic prognosis? Where in this life is peaceful contentment found when trouble abounds? Here is the answer: it is found in "seeing" what is beyond our human eyes to see, the eternal love of Jesus Christ. It is living by faith with an intimate relationship with the Lord. As the Book of Hebrews states, "Now faith is the assurance of things hoped for, the conviction of things *not* seen" (Hebrews 11:1, emphasis mine).

Seeing my life through the lens of God's love makes all the difference. Hope and contentment are found in seriously looking at what Jesus has done and is doing. He loved us when we were still sinful God-haters. His death and resurrection provided the only remedy to restore our relationship to God. He is the God of all comfort. He promises to take care of us each and every day.

True satisfaction, real contentment, can only be experienced by first being satisfied in the Lord himself. Focusing on Christ, and dwelling on all he has done for you, is the key to being content in all the seasons of your life. Note these inspiring words by John Piper:

> The burden of my ministry is to make plain to others that the "steadfast love [of the Lord] is better than life" (Psalm 63:3 RSV). If it is better than life, it is better than all that life in this world offers. This means that what satisfies are not the gifts of God, but the glory of God—the glory

of his love, the glory of his power, the glory of his wisdom, holiness, justice, goodness, and truth. . . This is why the psalmist Asaph cried out, "Whom have I in heaven but you? Besides you I desire nothing on earth. My flesh and my heart may fail, but God is the strength of my heart and my portion forever" (Psalm 73:25-26). Nothing on earth—none of God's good gifts of creation—could satisfy Asaph's heart. Only God could.[26]

This is a prayer for my own life, which I trust will encourage you as well: "Lord, help me to first and foremost find my satisfaction in you. Help me to rejoice in all you have done for me. Give me a deep sense of contentment in knowing I am loved by the Savior, so in turn I can be content in whatever troubles come my way. Help me to look beyond our medical circumstances and learn to be content in you. Amen."

Now let's look at some specific circumstances that can tempt us to be discontent and angry at the Lord. At the same time, let's also see the way to contentment through the power of Christ. I pray that you will find fresh hope as you read on.

Learning Contentment in Times of Trouble

Of the many memories I have of our years in Arizona, one thing I will never forget is the climate. Before leaving the green plush setting of upstate New York in the summer of 1991, I remember a friend of ours tried to give us a heads-up of what we were about to walk into. With just a hint of a smile he said, "It

"Learning Contentment"

is really hot there, but it is a *dry* heat. I'm sure you'll like it much better than the humidity here during the summer." Well, shortly after we arrived in Phoenix in July of 1991, I remember taking some time to browse at a clothing store at a north metro mall. As if positioned strategically just for me, a variety of shirts caught my attention proclaiming a very visual, detailed message. Several of these white shirts and tank tops had cartoon skeletons as their climate representative. I'll never forget seeing the image of a man of bones, golf cap positioned squarely on top of his skull, holding a beverage in a lawn chair. Above him was the caption, "Sure it's hot. But it is a dry heat." Yes, the time had arrived for us to enter into the furnace of southern Arizona.

As we lived through that first scorching summer, I knew I could now empathize with how chocolate chip cookie dough feels when it is thrust into the oven. A dry heat carries with it the power to "cook" anything that is willing to stand for very long in its presence. Over the years we experienced everything from burning our feet on concrete to seeing the kid's crayons transform into colorful puddles on the back seat of our car. We saw frozen ice cream become milkshake-like in just a few minutes as we drove home from the grocery store. Incredibly, one summer afternoon our windshield cracked under the strain of a high temperature of 120 degrees. The dog days of Arizona summers—you never see them advertised on their tourism commercials.

You'd think those searing days would have been monotonous and predictable—not so. For particularly in July and August the SPF-100-type days were capped off with incredible thunderstorms. The monsoon season, as it is called, often made late afternoons a blend of deafening thunder, horizontal lightning, gusty dust-filled winds, and brief torrential rains. The sudden transformation of weather was surreal. One minute I am trying to stay cool in the brilliant sunshine, and the next minute I am trying to safely ride out a powerful, violent storm.

I recall one late afternoon when one of these storms hit. Our white station wagon was inundated by pounding rain, car-rocking winds, and a brown sea of dirt so dense that I couldn't see the end of the hood of the car. Visibility went from miles to inches in seconds. I cautiously navigated our car off the road and into a parking space in an apartment complex. After about fifteen minutes of wind, rain, lightning and slimy brown dust, once again the sun appeared. In less than half an hour the clouds were gone. If it weren't for some muddy puddles hosting some blown leaves and twigs, you would hardly know the storm had even occurred.

I think it is beneficial to understand that living with chronic health issues is going to be a lot like an Arizona summer. Despite being already scorched by the daily hardship disease brings, other difficulties will come. Just because yourself or a loved one is ill doesn't mean you'll be exempt from the other storms of life. While dealing with the "heat" of disabling disease, other intense, personal monsoons will suddenly arrive. These added storms can tempt you to wonder if God really cares about all you are going through. You can easily feel overwhelmed—it can feel, as my friend Aaron likes to say, "Like the last straw, on top of the last straw, on top of the last straw." To deal with the searing nature of a disability or disease is a big load to carry. It is a gargantuan load to also have to face the "wind" of

"Learning Contentment"

parenting, the "downpour" of bills, and the "dust" of everything from home repairs to sinful attitudes.

C.H. Spurgeon, the renowned English pastor of the late nineteenth century, talked about how we, as Christians, have to accept the fact that our lives will have times of sunshine and darkness. Just as each day has a sunrise and sunset, so too each of us will have times of sunny prosperity and gloomy nighttime difficulty. We mustn't let it surprise us when, on top of our health battles, additional troubles come. He explains it this way:

> What then, my soul, is best for me to do? I must first learn to be content with God's divine order of things and be willing, just as Job was, to "accept good from God, and. . . trouble"(Job 2:10). Next, I must determine to have rejoicing flow from my life in the morning and the evening. I must praise the Lord for the sun of joy when it rises and for the gloom of evening as it falls. There is beauty in both the sunrise and sunset, so I should sing of it and glorify the Lord. Just as a nightingale does, I should sing at all hours and believe that the night is as useful as the day. The dew of God's grace falls most heavily during the night of sorrow, and His stars of promise shine most gloriously amid the darkness of grief.[27]

Regretfully, there have been several times in my life when I thought that Margaret's illness should be the only significant trial we should have to bear. When other, normal life challenges came our way, I would grumble and complain, thinking we deserved an exemption from such matters. After all, shouldn't a special "trial-free-card" come to a family already strained by the pressures of a chronic health condition? Isn't it right to think that there is already enough on our plate, and therefore we should be spared the typical challenges of life? Believe me, thinking this way will never bring the contentment to your heart that God desires. In my journey of learning contentment, the Lord has been showing me, through Christ, that contentment can be experienced even during the seasons of multiple troubles.

I would like to share with you some fairly recent trials we have experienced in addition to Margaret's illness. My goal is not to make you feel sorry for us. Rather, I think it is important for you to see that sickness often partners with other challenges. It is a distasteful reality in the world in which we live. Yet in the ocean of these troubles, our great God can give us the blessing of peace and contentment through Jesus.

Here's a list of some of the significant hardships we endured over a seventeen month period—this was the most difficult stretch of our lives:

•March 2010—Within five days of each other, Margaret's parents, Pete and Grace Aldrich, both passed away. Due to the limitations of Margaret's illness, we were unable to fly back to New York for their joint funeral.

•November 2010—Just six months after we had moved into our cozy ranch-style home, a dryer fire destroyed our laundry room and caused

"Learning Contentment"

extensive smoke damage. Though we escaped the nighttime blaze unharmed, we were displaced from our home for three months.

•February 2011—My older brother, John "Spark" Robble, died tragically at the age of 53. It was the saddest event of my life.

•June, July, and August 2011—Margaret was hospitalized three different times due to complications involving her disease and medications. The most serious of these hospital stays was in June, when a reaction to a prescribed medication caused her lungs to retain fluid.

During all these heart-wrenching circumstances, sarcoidosis was still a constant theme in our lives. Annoying symptoms still showed up every day. Now with the sarcoid discomforts came these extremely taxing events. With one big thing after another, I struggled with accepting what God was allowing in our lives. Some days contentment was miles away from my thinking. How can God expect us to be content when heavy waves of trouble keep coming? Aren't we justified to think now is the time to yell at God, tell him how much our life isn't fair, and then give him the pout-filled silent treatment? At times this path of distanced communication with the Lord seemed logical to me. In my anger (as you will read in chapter six), I did for a time withdraw from the Lord. But thank God, as the painful trials and their aftershocks multiplied, I realized how much I needed him to endure. No, now (and always for that matter) was the time to fall before God, plead with him for strength, and seek his peace and contentment.

As I am learning contentment, what I am seeing with more clarity is the path to contentment is making God my refuge in times of trouble. I cannot be satisfied in life unless I turn to the Lord, and find my strength and satisfaction in him. I must seek his face. I must cry out to him. I must see him as my only real hope in my times of distress. Please ponder these words of J.A. Motyer:

> The Psalmist wrote "Under his wings you will find refuge." (Psalm 91:4). . . Just as a chick runs to the mother hen for protection, so he runs to God. In the same way Paul, and we ourselves, are 'in Christ' by fleeing to him, pressing close to him, covering ourselves in him, hiding in him, by seeing the danger and taking shelter in him. Paul's experience of the trustworthiness of God can therefore be ours. We too can find ability to do all things (meet all circumstances with contentment) 'in' him who infuses us with dynamic power.[28]

Here is my experience: when I come to God in times of trouble, talk to him, cry before him, tell him all my desires and fears, and take time to read his promises— then I taste of his comforting presence. Then I find my heart becoming calm, with the contentment only God can provide. When I decide my additional trials are just too much, and I let my heart get angry with him, my soul becomes calloused—indifferent and cold toward the Lord. Soon bitterness, resentment, and discontentment, like a trio of criminal heart companions, rob me of the precious contentment and peace the Lord desires.

So, in those times when troubles multiply, let's make the Lord our refuge. Let's first and foremost look to him to find satisfaction in this life. Let's consistently escape to the shelter of his care, and find the reality of being content in all situations.

Learning Contentment Financially

I grew up in the era when TV was quite a bit different than it is today. From an equipment standpoint, there were no large flat screens with stadium-like surround sound. We had a color TV, but it sported the style of the sixties: dark brown wood cabinet, rounded square screen, and no remote controls. In fact, to change the channel or adjust the volume, one of us had to actually get up off the couch, and turn the appropriate knob on the front of our television. Yes, life was TV-rough back then. And channel choices? Only four—CBS, NBC, ABC and PBS. Our reception came via a large antenna that my dad had mounted to the roof of our house. There was no digital satellite dish, and no assortment of cable networks. Yes, those were the entertainment days of my youth, a time when most homes had one TV, and parents didn't have to worry much about what their kids were watching.

Despite the limited television choices back then, one show that did capture my attention was *Batman*. Though I didn't spend tons of time watching TV, *Batman* was a show I seldom missed. The Caped Crusader, in his black and grey attire, was weekly engaged in subduing the criminal behaviors of one of his archenemies. One week he would be faced with the antics of the Joker. Another week the Penguin was his nemesis. At times the Cat Woman or the Riddler would be his foe. Usually each program culminated in some type of hand-to-hand battle, where large animated words like "Pow!" or "Smash!" filled the screen as Batman let the bad guys have it.

Thankfully, Batman never had to take on these forces of evil alone. Robin, his reliable companion, was by his side, ready to take care of business with him. Robin's unique costume and boyish personality made him a perfect crime fighting partner. They were called the "Dynamic Duo" for a reason: together they had the power and the resources to take care of the villains, and make Gotham City safe once again.

In the world of chronic disease, there is also a dynamic duo of sorts. Unfortunately, this duo doesn't come to end the tyranny of sickness and disability. It doesn't arrive and powerfully bring needed relief to our medical circumstances. Instead of subduing the pain and strain, when it shows up it complicates things. Unlike Batman and Robin, its "Pow!" and "Smash!" is directed at us. It makes our lives even more difficult. What is this duo? It is the combo of illness and money pressures.

For me, the most persistent, consistent, and stressful pairing that comes with Margaret's sarcoidosis involves money. Providing for my family, and trying to pay for the unpredictable and often significant medical costs is a "Pow!", "Smash!", and "Bam!" that keeps me fervently praying to the Lord.

Please read carefully this not-so-encouraging quote from the NY Times.com:

"Learning Contentment"

Nearly two out of three bankruptcies stem from medical bills, and even people with health insurance face financial disaster if they experience a serious illness, a new study shows. . . The U.S. health care financing system is broken, and not only for the poor and uninsured. . . Middle-class families frequently collapse under the strain of a health care system that treats physical wounds, but often inflicts fiscal ones.[29]

As the article highlights, even with health insurance a serious illness can cause a family to "face financial disaster." As I mentioned in chapter one, we found ourselves in bankruptcy court in January of 2007. Sure, there were a number of financial decisions along the way that I wish I had done differently. I regret my sinful indifference and apathy when it came to managing our finances. But our reality was then and is now that Margaret's medical care costs us thousands of dollars each year.

Currently, to keep financially afloat I work a few part-time jobs in addition to my regular full-time teaching position. During the school year I spend a few hours a week providing one-on-one math tutoring. I work every Saturday from 6:45 a.m. to noon as a manager at a nearby retirement community. Each year from early June to mid-July I teach summer school. By God's grace we have enough income to keep our home, have food on the table, and keep weathering the monthly challenge of medical bills.

Yet there is always a temptation to be discontent, to envy those who don't see their income drain into the endless stream of medical costs. Recently I heard of a family that was going to the beach in Mexico on a two week vacation. Immediately my mind began to wonder how fun two weeks at the beach would be for our family. I also felt the strong temptation to question the wisdom of God's plan for us, since our sarcoidosis journey doesn't allow the liberty to pack our bags for a time of fun in the surf and sun. Typically a chronic illness doesn't allow the mobility or extra financial resources for things like special vacations. Like it or not, most left-over cash needs to go for life's essentials, not recreational adventures. So once again I had to seek the Lord, and remind myself of the blessings of my salvation. I had to tell my soul that we are a blessed family, not because of the funds in our bank account, but because of the Lord's never-ending love and care for us.

Thank God, here is the biblical truth to confess and cling to: (yes, I am going to say it one more time). . . The Lord's perspective of you and me is not based on our medical or financial circumstances. His favor and love for us is based on what Christ has done for us. "There is therefore now no condemnation for those who are in Christ Jesus" (Romans 8:1). Nothing "will be able to separate us from the love of God in Christ Jesus our Lord" (Romans 8:39). Remember—you can be living in the goodness and power of the gospel and be physically sick with depleted finances. Yes, our bank accounts can be drained, we may lose our jobs, and disease and disability may persist in our lives. This isn't an indication that God is upset with us, and is somehow circumstantially showing us his displeasure. God's love for you and me is based on what Jesus has accomplished. "God shows his love for us in that while we were still sinners, Christ died for us" (Romans 5:8).

"Learning Contentment"

It is possible (and frankly probable) that suffering of all kinds, including disease and money problems, will come to many of us who are following the Lord.

From my experience, when money problems join forces with Margaret's medical symptoms, the stage is set to see the Lord's strength in a special way. The overwhelming nature of it all drives me to my knees. I feel incredibly weak and helpless. I see in a deep way how life is too hard to live without a Savior. I passionately cry out to God and tell him all about my troubles and fears. I pray for his divine enablement to be grateful and content. And, in my weakness, I am strengthened by his amazing grace. Though it is far from fun, it is richly spiritually beneficial. I see his love for me and my family in a very personal and tangible way. I taste of his miraculous presence, peace, and contentment.

What I continue to be reminded of is that true contentment can only be found in Christ. When, by his grace, satisfaction is rooted in the Savior, there is immense benefit. Note this inspiring passage of scripture, found in 1 Timothy 6:6-8:

> Now there is great gain in godliness with contentment, for we brought nothing into this world, and we cannot take anything out of the world. But if we have food and clothing, with these we will be content.

I'd like to take a few moments to focus on some of the key truths found in these verses. As I do, I pray the Lord will encourage your heart to be content regardless of your financial circumstances. To begin, I think it will be helpful to read how the *Amplified Bible* phrases this passage:

> [And it is, indeed, a source of immense profit, for] godliness accompanied with contentment (that contentment which is a source of inward sufficiency) is great and abundant gain. For we brought nothing into the world, and *obviously* we cannot take anything out of the world; But if we have food and clothing, with these we shall be content (satisfied).[30]

Let's begin by digging into the opening phrase, "there is *great gain* (i.e. immense profit) in godliness with contentment." As I pondered this verse, I felt it would be beneficial to draw from my New Testament Greek class, which I took in college way back in 1981. (Yes, I do still remember some of what I was taught, and yes, we did have electricity back then.) The word translated "great" comes from the Greek word "megos." In the English language, this is where the prefix "mega" comes from, which means "large. . . or a million."[31] For example, a megaton explosion is equivalent to 1,000,000 tons of TNT.

Now let this sink in. Godly, Christ-honoring contentment is of "mega-gain." It is hugely profitable, almost beyond measure. Greater than a prosperous financial portfolio is having Christ-like character with contentment. God places a high priority in being satisfied in him. With chronic disease our finances may become strained. The accumulation of our monthly bills may overwhelm our paycheck. If with God's help, however, we can stay close to the Lord with a thankful attitude

"Learning Contentment"

of contentment, the benefit in our lives will be great. Of infinitely more value than financial security is God-security. When money challenges come, having him as our joy and satisfaction makes all the difference. Let's honor God by being people of character, who see him as our refuge at all times, whether money is tight or is in abundance.

When the duo of sickness and money pressures arrive, usually I am immediately tempted to complain. Anxiety again lurks to get a foothold in my soul, and the troubles of my life can quickly seem too big to handle. If I yield to sin, allowing my heart to murmur, getting worried about how we will make it through the month, and wondering why on top of our health issues we now have money woes, our trials get much more complicated. The reality of God's peace and provision become clouded to me. I get much more irritable with Margaret and the children. Bitterness again begins to try to rear its ugly head. My sinful attitudes just make the whole situation worse.

But, what incredible gain there is when, by God's grace I am content. When the temptations come, if I quickly cry out to God, he strengthens me. He gives me peace. He blesses me with hope, and an assurance he will take care of me and my family. He gives me wisdom and direction. The Lord in the middle of financial struggles makes all the difference. I am "mega-helped." I am "mega-strengthened." I experience "great" gain through the provision of Christ. Is your heart in turmoil due to money pressures pressing on top of your medical trials? Seek the Lord. Ask him to help you learn to be content no matter what your financial circumstances.

He will help you to experience the immense benefit of his comforting presence.

Secondly, let's remember that "we brought *nothing* into this world, and we *cannot take anything* out of the world." When you and I were born, we had no bank accounts, no retirement fund, no cozy home of our own in the suburbs. We came onto this planet naked, and totally dependent on others to provide for our needs. So too on the day of our death, no earthly possessions go with us. Everything, materially speaking, we have purchased or earned will be left behind. It is so important to see our material things as temporary. The reality is that we have no lasting hold on what we own. Ultimately our income and possessions really belong to God, and he can use them as he pleases. So, if a high percentage of my paychecks go for medical treatments instead of comforting material things, so be it. None of my stuff is going with me anyway. I must live with the realization that what is most vital, what really defines my success, isn't what I own. What is most important is the person I am in Christ.

Finally, "if we have *food* and *clothing*, with these we will be content." This is the part of the passage where I can start to feel a bit uncomfortable. I am happy to embrace the verse about the great gain of godliness with contentment. Sure, I can nod my head in agreement with the truth that all my possessions are temporary. Being content with just food and clothes, however, seems a bit extreme. What about my hard work to get to a place of financial security? Don't we live in America, where each of us is entitled to a slice of the American dream? Shouldn't it be true that if I work hard, am a man of good character, and keep

"Learning Contentment"

striving towards my material wishes, eventually I will have what I want?

The truth is, even with godly character and a good work ethic, chronic disease will most likely readjust your material wishes and financial goals. When faced with an ongoing illness or disability, we need to keep looking at our resources from a needs perspective. Some material things, though enjoyed by many, may not be feasible for the family dealing with healthcare costs. Particularly over the past few years I have had to redefine what our needs really are, based on the teaching of scripture. The Lord promises to provide for us the essentials of life: food and shelter. He doesn't guarantee us many of the things that as a culture we have come to expect. The Apostle Paul learned contentment "facing plenty and hunger, abundance and need" (Philippians 4:12). As families dealing with illness and medical costs, we too must understand we will be facing times of monetary "hunger" and "need." Yet during these times, we can trust God to take care of us and see us through.

Though it hasn't been easy, over the years I have had to make numerous financial adjustments. I have had to redefine our financial goals, and adjust our budget to be able to pay for healthcare costs. I have to work some long days to provide for my family. I have found myself curbing our desire to buy nonessential things. I have had to say "No" more often to our teenage children. When the time came to get their driver's licenses, for example, both of our kids understood they had to help pay for their car insurance. Most of their friends' parents paid the entire cost for the added insurance—not so in our household. Funds must be managed closely to ensure our needs are taken care of. This is our healthcare-permeated fiscal reality.

Thankfully, with the assistance of sound financial counseling, I am growing in clarity on what a needs-orientated financial perspective looks like. Yes, some American "dream-like" items have had to go. Yet with their removal has also come added peace and contentment. Though I still have much to learn, I thank God he is faithfully helping me to understand and experience financial contentment in the midst of our circumstances.

Some Concluding Thoughts on Contentment

For the chronically ill and their families, learning contentment is going to be an ongoing struggle. Like it or not, your life will be radically different than most folks. Your daily routine will be different. Your relationships will be altered. Your financial goals will be changed. A medical trial will shake your world, reconfiguring your life in ways you never could have imagined.

Like us, you will probably face learning contentment in a multitude of areas not mentioned in this chapter. When you are tempted to envy and complain, remember the Savior. He is able to give you satisfaction no matter what your circumstances. As I have already discussed in chapter four, it is such a blessing to know God understands the chronic illness world. He can meet the deepest needs of your soul.

Yes, with all the change, hardship, and uniqueness of your health battle, God is in control. He is the master teacher of contentment. As I conclude this chapter, once again I am reminded of what Christ did when he

"Learning Contentment"

came to earth. Consider this incredible verse found in 2 Corinthians 8:9: "For you know the grace of our Lord Jesus Christ, that though he was rich, yet for your sake he became poor, so that you by His poverty might become rich."

When I reflect on this verse, and think about what Jesus has done, it stirs gratefulness in my heart. Christ left the riches of heaven, became man, and paid the price for my sins. Because of his love for me, my soul now knows his forgiveness, his strength, and his power to endure. Margaret is healthy in spirit because she knows the Savior who cares for her and died on the cross for her. We have Christ's help and comfort. We are learning and experiencing contentment because of his abounding love for us. Sure, our troubles may multiply at times, but we are rich because of Jesus. May God continue to deepen our love for him and our satisfaction in him in the days ahead.

Discussion Questions

1) Define what contentment means. Would you describe yourself as a content person? Why or why not?
2) Where is true, biblical contentment found?
3) What are the areas in your life where you need to grow in contentment? How do you anticipate God helping you to be more content?

Chapter Six

"Practical Encouragements"

"How much better to get wisdom than gold! To get understanding is to be chosen rather than silver" (Proverbs 16:16).

Olympic distance runner and 1972 gold medalist Frank Shorter was once quoted as saying, "You don't run 26 miles at five minutes a mile on good looks and a secret recipe."[32] His clear message here is there is no substitute for purposeful, sacrificial, and grueling training. Sweat, sweat, and more sweat are to be the expectation of the marathoner. The runner must wisely train, readying himself for the long, difficult race ahead.

Like it or not, a chronic disease or disability thrusts a family into a medical marathon. For us, the past twenty-five years have paralleled the route of a challenging distance race. There have been some smoother, less strenuous years, when pounding the medical pavement didn't seem too bad. Other years have been like running up an endless hill with its crest hidden in the

"Practical Encouragements"

fog. Exhausted, our souls being winded with relentless medical pressures, we trudged on, not knowing when the steep slope would transition to more bearable, level ground. Often along the way, when our fatigue tempted us to lose hope and quit, we have felt the cool refreshment of God, watering our souls and quenching our deepest spiritual thirst. Re-energized to continue in the race, we kept pressing forward, though we had no idea what additional obstacles waited for us around the next corner. Yes, it has been a long and often unpredictable medical journey. Even as I write today, Margaret sleeps in our bed, battling an infection in her arm. Once again her compromised immune system has been victimized. To be sure, our illness-permeated distance race has no visible finish line.

The reality is that normal family life swiftly fades away when health challenges appear. Conditions that are chronic and incurable become the catalysts of a new life frequently consumed by patient care and medical treatments. Patients and their families face not miles, but years of emotional toil and perseverance trying to make the best of their limitations and challenges. In order to run such a long-term race successfully, help is needed. As has already been discussed, first and foremost, the patient and caregiver will need the support and care that only God can give. A personal, saving relationship with the Lord through faith in Christ is essential. They will need to prayerfully embrace Bible-centered doctrine. They will need to consistently seek the Lord about all the issues that come with medical trials.

Yet knowing, seeking, and following God in and of itself is not enough. Wise practical decisions will need to be made. Prudent routines will need to be put in place. Most of these decisions and routines are going to require the support of other people. Gleaning from the wisdom of others is going to be crucial. Getting help, particularly during the more difficult times, will be invaluable.

I used to think me and God, my personal dynamic duo, could handle anything. It sounded so manly, so spiritually macho. I figured I had the Lord, and the power of his Holy Spirit, so that made me a superman of sorts. Going to other people with my troubles felt like a sign of weakness. After all, as an American Christian, shouldn't I show the world how amazing God is, by demonstrating how Jesus and me can handle anything?

This kind of independent thinking may sound appealing, but it isn't biblical. In order to endure the challenges of a medical trial (or any trial for that matter) you are going to need the help of others. My superman mentality never worked for long. The multiplicity of troubles quickly became kryptonite to my soul. Life was too hard. I just couldn't bear the severity of the burden alone. I needed help, sent from God, through people. As we shall see, the Lord never intended any Christian to battle his troubles apart from others. A primary means of God's love and care is designed to come your way through other believers.

Frank Shorter didn't win his gold medal by isolating himself, and gleaning self-inspired motivation. The intense process of getting ready for the Olympics required the support of others. He wasn't on some athletic island. He, like all of us, needed direction and encouragement along the way.

"Practical Encouragements"

A key part of his Olympic success had to do with his coach, Bob Giegengack. As his senior track season at Yale approached, Shorter asked Giegengack about his potential as a distance runner.

> His legendary mentor told him he could have a future in running. Encouraged by the response, Shorter redoubled his efforts, training harder than ever before for his last year of collegiate competition. . . He may have been the nation's most improved runner that year. . . [This] led Shorter to pursue his Olympic dreams, dreams that had been nurtured by Giegengack, the coach of 1964 U.S. Olympic track team. [33]

Giegengack was in Shorter's corner, nurturing him, encouraging him, and inspiring him to become the best marathon runner in the world. Shorter would never have reached the success he had without his coach, and others who helped him along the way. Independence would have kept him from Olympic gold. To earn the ultimate track prize, Frank Shorter knew he needed to lean on others whose experience and expertise would fuel his passion and dreams.

As Christians, God does not want us facing our medical challenges alone. He wants us first to know that he fully understands all we are going through. Jesus truly and intimately can relate to everything that goes with our pain and suffering. He also wants to enrich our lives by sending us special people as messengers of hope and provision. For us, these relationships have been priceless. The support, prayer, and encouragement we continue to receive make all the difference. I honestly don't believe we could have endured all the years of our medical troubles without God's gift of friends.

Where can you find these kind of friends? Where can you get not only practical help in your struggles, but also spiritual support and encouragement? Your family? Maybe. Neighbors? Possibly. Co-workers? Could be. But ultimately, the Lord wants to bless you through a local church. "Me, with all my troubles, joining a local church," you say? Yes. It is God's will. Whether you realize it or not, you need them, and they need you.

Join a Church that Inspires You to Persevere

"I will build my church, and the gates of hell shall not prevail against it" (Matthew 16:18b).

As I begin this section, I realize you may be one of many who have lived through a difficult church experience. Your personal docudrama, staged in a local church setting, may have left you scarred and disillusioned. Possibly as a result of what you went through, you decided to never give church a chance again. No way do you want to bring your life, with all its health challenges and complexities, back to those Christian folk. Your church wounds may have gone deep and their resultant scars are hard to ignore. So, to play it safe you have decided to make the best of your medical ordeal with as little Christian interaction as possible. Why complicate everything by taking a risk, and putting your heart out there for others to see?

Years ago someone told me, "Mike, if you ever find a perfect church, don't join it." His point was clear: if a

"Practical Encouragements"

perfect church did exist, my sinful imperfections would ruin it. Obviously there are no perfect churches. We as Christians still sin. Church life can be messy and difficult, leaving in its wake wounded people. Margaret and I have been bruised a few times over the years in our relationships with other Christians. But despite the setbacks that may come, the Lord wants his people plugged into local churches. Yes, even with the imperfections of churches, and the independent mindset our culture promotes, we are created to live our lives with the help of others. It is God's idea. As believers in Christ, we need the other members of his body, and they need us. God didn't save us to live our lives in isolation from our fellow believers. He has positioned and gifted us to be a part of his body, the church. Note these amazing verses found in 1 Corinthians 12:12,14-26:

> For just as the body is one and has many members, and all the members of the body, though many, are one body, so it is with Christ. . . For the body does not consist of one member but of many. If the foot should say, "Because I am not a hand, I do not belong to the body," that would not make it any less a part of the body. And if the ear should say, "Because I am not an eye, I do not belong to the body," that would not make it any less a part of the body. If the whole body were an eye, where would be the sense of hearing? If the whole body were an ear, where would be the sense of smell? But as it is, God arranged the members of the body, each one of them, as he chose. If all were a single member, where would the body be? As

it is, there are many parts, yet one body. The eye cannot say to the hand, "I have no need of you," nor again the head to the feet, "I have no need of you." On the contrary, the parts of the body that seem to be weaker are indispensible, and on those parts of the body that we think less honorable we bestow the greater honor, and our unpresentable parts are treated with greater modesty, which our presentable parts do not require. But God has so composed the body, giving greater honor to the part that lacked it, that there may be no division in the body, but that the members may have the same care one for another. If one member suffers, all suffer together; if one member is honored, all rejoice together.

Why have I inserted such a lengthy passage of scripture? Because it is so vital, particularly as Christians dealing with chronic health issues, that we understand the position we have been given in the body of Christ. If you are a Christian, you have a new identity in Jesus. God calls you a "new creation" (2 Corinthians 5:17). Incredibly, as new creations in Christ, we are now and forever "children of God" (Romans 8:16). Yes, we have left the court room, fearing the judgment of God, and have been placed into God's family room. A Christian is a son or daughter of God himself. Forever your adoption has been finalized. He is your Father, both now and for all of eternity (note Romans 8:15). You are a permanent member of God's family, eternally fused into the body of Christ.

"Practical Encouragements"

As I think about this divine, miraculous reality of being in the body of Christ, it flashes me back to our children's adoptions. All the paperwork, home visits, phone calls, fees, etc, paled on the day we stood in court. As we entered into the courtroom, our anticipation spilled into happy, nervous laughter. Family and friends joined us in our glee, knowing that in a few short minutes the life-changing transaction was about to occur. As the proceedings were about to begin, the judge, cloaked in his traditional black robe, had a cheerful glisten in his eyes. We stood a few feet in front of him, dressed in our Sunday best. I positioned myself to Margaret's left, as she held our baby gently in her arms. Our lawyer, happy and looking a bit weary from his labor, stood to Margaret's right. This was the moment we had all been waiting for.

After a few minutes of formality (we had to answer some standard adoption questions), the judge was ready to make his legal pronouncements. First he declared that our child now had a new name. This decree had nothing to do with DNA. It was based on the judicial transaction that accompanies adoption. On each of their respective days, both our daughter and son became official members of the Robble family, and their new name proved it. Then the judge firmly but joyfully proclaimed, "I declare that the relationship between this couple and this child will be forever parent and child." As the tears of joy welled out of our eyes, we knew that our family had just been amazingly blessed and permanently transformed. The new member of the Robble family was now legally sealed and secured.

Always Sick, Always Loved

When God saves you, a similar legal proceeding takes place. You are given a new, spiritual birth (John 3:1-8). You are declared righteous, justified in God's sight by the atoning work of Christ (Galatians 2:15-16). And, having been justified, God adopts you. He is forever your Father. You are forever his son or daughter. You have been welcomed, sealed, and secured into the family of God. And guess what? You now have a multiplicity of brothers and sisters in Christ—spiritual relatives prepared by the Lord to enrich and benefit your life. There is a group of Christian siblings the Lord wants you to be close to. They are to be found at the local church he wants you to be a part of. God's desire is they get to know you, and you get to know them. He wants your relationships to grow, and as a result you will mutually care for each other. The Lord doesn't want you suffering alone; he desires to bless you through his life in others.

With this incredible reality in mind, let's focus on some of the key points in the passage from 1 Corinthians 12. First of all, you belong. You can't say "I do not belong to the body." Your medical troubles, and all that goes with them, doesn't nullify your God-given position in the body of Christ. Whether you think you don't fit in or even if others don't feel you belong, God has placed you in his body "as he chose." Don't entertain the thought for a moment that you and your family shouldn't be a part of a local church. Meditate on your wonderful biblical reality— being in Christ has made you worthy to be in Jesus' church.

Secondly, (and this is my favorite) you are "indispensable" to the body of Christ. I love how the *Amplified Bible* expresses this thought: "there is [absolute]

"Practical Encouragements"

necessity for the parts of the body that are considered more weak."[34] Feeling weak and overwhelmed in your circumstances? Do you see yourself going to a church service as maybe the neediest person in the congregation? Are you so overwhelmed and consumed in your medical troubles you wonder how you could ever possibly be a blessing to others? God says you are a necessary, important, indispensable, member of his body. You are an essential part of your Christian family. You need your fellow church members, and they need you.

For us, it has been life-changing to embrace and apply this truth. Margaret's illness has not made her a second or third class Christian. Her disease has not demoted her or our family to a lower level of Christendom. On the contrary, in the Lord's sight we are just as worthy to be in his body as any other believer. As hard as it may be for us to believe (but we must, because it is scriptural) we are indispensable. We are not the high maintenance family that few want to know because of all the baggage we bring with us. We are vital and needful to the well-being of the body of Christ. . . and so are you.

Finally, fellow Christians are being prepared by God to "suffer together" with you. God wants to give you the gift of people who will come alongside, show godly compassion, and help you along the way. Over the years we have experienced over and over expressions of love and support through our church family. Prayers, words of encouragement, financial gifts, meals, rides for the children, timely visits, help maintaining our home, and a host of other acts of kindness have flowed into our lives. The Lord has abundantly blessed us with wonderful people who have considered it a joy to be our friends.

These friends are God's ambassadors of love to us. Even though Margaret is no longer able to attend church functions, the relationships I enjoy in our church have linked her to our church family as well. Care for me has spilled over into abundant care for her. It is the miracle of God's provision through his body. . . And, as a Christian patient or caregiver, this is the Lord's desire for you as well.

Thank God, the Lord consistently uses our brothers and sisters in Christ to comfort us and remind us of his care for us. As I think about our local church, I am overwhelmed with gratitude as I consider all the blessings we have received. I know if I started writing about these blessings in any detail this section would grow into a chapter of its own. My point is this: God wants to bless you and your family through a local church. You will be on the receiving end, and you will also have the joy of being on the giving end. It is real, living Christianity.

Yes, you, as a Christian, now have the privilege of joining a church in your community. It is what God intends for you and your family to bring the added love and support you need. He wants you to move forward by faith and see and experience all he has for you through involvement in a church. Consider these words by J.I. Packer:

The New Testament assumes that all Christians will share in the life of a local church, meeting with it for worship (Heb. 10:25), accepting its nurture and discipline (Matt. 18:15-20; Gal. 6:1), and sharing its work of witness. Christians

"Practical Encouragements"

disobey God and impoverish themselves by refusing to join with other believers when there is a local congregation that they can belong to.[35]

With all I have said so far, I pray the Lord is helping you to understand how important it is to be involved with the family of God. I passionately believe the Lord wants to break the cycle of loneliness for the chronically ill and their families. It is hard enough to suffer day in and day out in the world of disabling disease. Yet to go week after week with few if any friends to support you makes your challenges harder. The Lord desires to send others to help bear your burdens (note Galatians 6:2). I believe God wants to lead you to a church where you can be consistently loved and cared for. He desires to give you Christ-centered friendships, people you can be real with and cry with, without fear of being judged. By faith he wants you to prayerfully find your local church family. I pray the Lord will give you the courage and the grace to connect with your brothers and sisters in Christ in your community.

As you begin your church-finding journey, I wish I could say all churches are created equal. I wish I could tell you that if *Jesus* is written on the church sign all will be well. Unfortunately, this is not the case. All churches are not the same. So, you will need a set of biblical criteria to apply as you look for a church. What are these criteria? I think the best place to look is in Acts 2:42-47:

And they devoted themselves to the apostles' teaching and the fellowship, to the breaking of bread and the prayers. And awe came upon every soul, and many wonders and signs were

Always Sick, Always Loved

being done through the apostles. And all who believed were together and had all things in common. And they were selling their possessions and belongings and distributing the proceeds to all, as any had need. And day by day, attending the temple together and breaking bread in their homes, they received their food with glad and generous hearts, praising God and having favor with all the people. And the Lord added to their number day by day those who were being saved.

I believe these key traits in Acts 2 about the church at Jerusalem provide a helpful template in your search for a church family. We have applied them to help us discern what church the Lord would have us join. I am grateful that our current church, Grace Community Church in Westminster, Colorado, passionately seeks to emulate these truths. As a church we haven't arrived by any means. We are growing in our understanding of what a New Testament church should be. But the fruit of this biblical foundation is evident—and it is why we are happy to say we are members of GCC.

Now let's take a closer look at these verses. The first key truth presented is a theological one, and it must be the preeminent standard for choosing a church. The church at Jerusalem was "devoted to the apostles teaching." First and above all else, dig deep into what a church believes. Find out the key details of their biblical foundation. As I discussed in chapter three, right doctrine leads to sound living. The litmus test for determining the church you join must be first focused on what the church believes about God and the Bible.

"Practical Encouragements"

Is the church you are considering gospel-centered? Does it exalt and proclaim Jesus and his atoning work above everything else? Do the pastors teach what the Bible does regarding suffering and sickness? Ask your potential pastor what he believes about Christ and the gospel. Ask him about his theology of suffering. See if the church's foundation is Christ and their theology is based on the teachings of scripture. This must be priority number one.

Secondly, if theologically the church is biblical, look at the corporate dynamic of the church. Is there evidence the folks are "devoted" to the truths being taught, and to "fellowship, to the breaking of bread and [to] prayer?" During worship times, do you feel uplifted and drawn closer to God? Are you sensing spiritual encouragement to persevere in your health challenges? Do you see evidence of their care for each another? Is there a measure of sincere warmth, common vision, and generosity? Are people welcoming toward you and your family, and do you feel they are passionate about their relationship with Christ? On the practical side, is there some type of small group ministry that will provide a context for you to build godly relationships with others? As you are given opportunities, do you have a desire to get to know them as your brothers and sisters in Christ?

I'd encourage you to keep praying for the Lord's leading. Ask him to give you discernment to know which church you should join. Keep the criteria in Acts 2 before you. Take your time, but don't drag your feet. God wants to comfort you through his people. Since he promises to lead you "in paths of righteousness for his name's sake" (Psalm 23:3), I am confident he will bring you to your church family, and because of his direction and blessing, you will be better equipped to persevere down the tough road of chronic disease.

I'd now like to go on to my next practical encouragement, which has a clear connection to your local church: cultivating your personal relationship with God. Do you desire a more intimate life with your Savior? Do you want to grow in your understanding of all you have been given through the love of Christ? Please read on, and I pray the Lord will help you in this key aspect of your Christian life.

<u>Cultivate Your Personal Relationship With God</u>

"Like newborn infants, long for the pure spiritual milk, that by it you may grow up to salvation—if indeed you have tasted that the Lord is good" (1 Peter 2:2-3).

During my years growing up in upstate New York, I always enjoyed the summer visits I had with my grandparents. They lived in a modest, gray two-story home, the same house where they had raised their three daughters (one of which is my mom). Flanked by a couple of acres of land and tall, stoic trees, I always found their home warm and inviting. Typically when I came over Grandma would lovingly offer me a cool drink complemented by a homemade treat. She loved spending time in her kitchen, and the steady waft of flavorful aromas in their house confirmed it. Something was always simmering or baking, and my palate reaped the benefits.

"Practical Encouragements"

My grandfather's preferred place was his garden. This was his retirement office of sorts, a place where caring for plants gave him a deep sense of pride and accomplishment. He loved to spend hours meticulously grooming rows of potatoes, corn, cucumbers, tomatoes, and an array of other vegetables. With sweat dripping from the base of his wavy gray hair, Gramps would delight to show me the fruit of his labor, naming and pointing out the sturdy, well-watered greenery.

He was a master gardener. Grandpa knew what each type of plant needed, and what would hinder its fruitfulness. His care began with the right fertilizer—no chemicals here. Gramps fed his plants a homemade compost mixture, a fragrant combination of assorted rotting foliage. Complementing the fertilizer was the right amount of moisture. Daily he would walk across the street, two large five gallon pails in hand, to scoop up fresh water from nearby Bradley Creek. With the full pails stretching his arms below his waist, he would plop them down next to his garden, and then carefully pour the appropriate amount of water near the base of each plant. None of grandpa's veggies were under or over watered. He made sure each and every one got the right amount of moisture they needed. Weeds also had no place in his garden. Any foreign green invader was quickly targeted and yanked. Ironically, the dead weeds final resting place was in the latest version of his compost pile—they would actually be a part of the next serving of garden fertilizer.

By the end of each summer the abundance of vegetables that came out of that small parcel of land was amazing. My grandmother would make home-made pickles, freeze fresh corn, and can enough veggie-related supplies to last all winter. I can still remember eating their frozen sweet corn (at times it was a side dish with roasted rabbit—I am not kidding—I never could eat a prepared hare) in the middle of January. The yellow kernels, cut fresh off the cob in August, still had that succulent fresh corn taste.

In a similar fashion to how Grandpa cared for his garden, God desires for every Christian to cultivate their personal relationship with him. He desires that our lives with Christ be strong, nourished in the proper way. He wants our souls well-watered, so that we can successfully weather all the seasons of our lives. He wants us to be protected from any of life's "weeds" that can take root and choke our relationship with him. As a result, the Lord desires to use our lives to "bear much fruit and so prove to be [his] disciples" (John 15:8).

You see, one of the wonders of Christianity is that it is a living relationship with a living God. You and I can experience intimacy with Christ. We can taste of his presence. We can sit at his feet and be strengthened in the knowledge of who he is, and the infinite love he has for us. The Lord desires for us to experience this reality: "Draw near to God, and he will draw near to you" (James 4:6).

The Lord wants you and me to be growing in our understanding of who he is, and who we are in Christ. A key aspect of our Christian life is learning more and more about the incredible love the Savior has for us. As the Lord helps us to build our relationship with him, we will be more amazed about our salvation. We will be more confident in his unchanging love for us. We will be more secure in his mysterious, sovereign plan. We

"Practical Encouragements"

will want to love, honor and serve him more. Our passion can begin to reflect the desire Paul exclaimed in Philippians 3:10: "That I may know him and power of his resurrection, and may share his sufferings, becoming like him in his death." Like in any relationship, however, a purposeful plan and energy will be required. We will need to make wise soul-strengthening choices.

Please be mindful that all I am about to share is *significantly* enriched by being a part of a local church. You need the life of Christ in other believers to ensure your soul is well cared for. There exists a corporate component of cultivating your relationship with the Lord that cannot be ignored. If you want your soul well nourished, you must be a part of a Christ-centered church. So, lest I repeat too much from what I have already shared, be prepared to see references to church life and ministry—there is a direct correlation to growing in your relationship with the Lord and being connected to your local church.

Though there is a vast amount of material that could be written on this topic, I'd like to capsulate it into three key areas: worship, Bible intake, and prayer. These are the *Big Three* nourishments of my soul, each complemented by the relationships and ministries I benefit from at Grace Community Church. Let's begin by looking into worship, and leaning again on the wisdom provided by J.I. Packer:

> Worship in the Bible is the due respect of rational creatures to the self-revelation of their Creator. . . It involves praising him for what he is, thanking him for what he has done, desiring him to get himself more glory by further acts

of mercy, judgment, and power, and trusting him with our concern for our own and others' future well-being. Moods of awestruck wonder and grateful celebration are all part of it."[36]

Worship is an attitude of the heart. It often comprises humming, singing, and thanking God out loud. Today, for example, as I was trekking through the aisles at a local grocery store, I was singing a worship song. I wasn't singing very loud, but there, surrounded by vast amounts of food, produce and supplies, I was expressing gratitude to the Lord. Why? It had been a bit of a difficult day. I received a few more medical bills in the mail, Margaret wasn't feeling very well, and my allergies had sent me a dull sinus headache. I was weary, and found myself feeling beaten down by the day's challenges. So, with God's help, I sang to my Savior. As I gazed at the grocery list and methodically placed items in my shopping cart, I worshipped the One who gives me strength. The result? My soul was reminded of Christ's love for me. My heart was blessed with fresh peace and hope. Worship helped me to remember the faithfulness of the Lord.

I don't understand how it all works, but worshipping the Lord helps my soul keep a biblical perspective. When I sing to the Lord, I get renewed strength. Sometimes I praise him for his promises. Other times I thank him for all he has done for us, particularly for his miracle of perseverance. My goal is to focus my soul heavenward, and thank God for the richness of my salvation. Margaret does the same. She frequently is humming and singing songs to the Lord despite all her pain and disabling affliction. She knows God is helping

"Practical Encouragements"

her, and wants him to hear her gratitude through song. Her worship is a living example to me of God's grace and love. It inspires me to pray that we will continue to grow in our understanding of worship, and its importance in our lives. Might we, from the depths of our hearts say with the Psalmist, "Praise the Lord! For it is good to sing praises to our God; for it is pleasant, and a song of praise is fitting" (Psalm 147:1).

A huge exclamation point to individual worship is corporate worship. I love praising God with my brothers and sisters in Christ at our Sunday church services. I also am edified by worshipping with them at our smaller care group meetings. In both contexts I am consistently encouraged. I receive intimate spiritual strength. My heart is drawn closer to the Lord and closer to my fellow believers. Often God speaks to my deepest needs and hurts when I am worshipping with my brothers and sisters in Christ. I have experienced over and over again the benefit of "singing psalms and hymns and spiritual songs" (Colossians 3:16b) with my Christian friends. How I thank God for the avenue of worship! It is a key part of cultivating my relationship with the Lord.

Now let's proceed to the second of the *Big Three*: Bible intake. To introduce this, I'd like to talk about food. My purpose is not to get you longing for some tasty culinary creation seen on some cable food channel. I won't be quoting some renowned TV chef, providing for you the specifics on how to cook a delicious meal. Rather, I think there is a close correlation between physical food and spiritual food. You see, if I neglect nutrition for my body, I tend to be quite irritable—just ask Margaret. Some of my worst displays of sinful, angry frustration have appeared during my times of hunger. Lack of sustenance plays a part in turning me into a Jekyll and Hyde Christian. I don't blame the lack of protein and carbohydrates. It is my sin. But the temptation to be angry and easily annoyed is greatly enhanced if I skip a meal. So when I feel strong pangs of hunger, I need to pray. I must ask God to help me be kind and patient while my stomach growls. I know without a regular intake of food I am much more inclined to sin.

Thankfully, Margaret is a great cook. This helps explain why during the first year we were married I gained forty pounds. Her culinary gift helped transform me from a 128 pound stick-man to what I am today (and yes, I have gone a bit too far in the other direction—you won't be seeing me on any fitness magazine covers). Gleaning from her mom's kitchen training, she creates healthy, made from scratch meals and desserts. When I eat Margaret's cooking, I am satisfied. The temptation to be Mr. Grumpy is reduced. Good eating makes a difference—I feel more at peace, and my body has the fuel it needs to complete the tasks before me.

In a similar way, God wants his children being fed healthy spiritual food. This food is the word of God. As the Psalmist said, "I will meditate on your precepts and fix my eyes on your ways. I will delight in your statutes; I will not forget your word" (Psalm 119:15-16). Paul told the Colossian church to "let the word of Christ dwell in you richly, teaching and admonishing one another in all wisdom" (Colossians 3:16a). Just like our bodies need good nutrition to help them function properly, our souls need a steady, healthy diet of scripture. The Bible is where you will find your soul fuel. Neglecting

"Practical Encouragements"

the word of God will, over time, make you a malnour- ished Christian.

When I neglect reading the Bible, my soul is weak. My troubles soon seem bigger than God's ability to take care of them. I easily forget who I am in Christ. I can lose sight of God's passionate love for me. I find myself deprived of the deep-seated awareness of the Lord's care and provision for me and my family. God feels farther away, which makes me feel like I have been left to fend for myself. I just don't have much to say to my soul when life's cares confront me. My faith now seems more like a cold religion, not a personal relationship with a risen Savior.

This is why, on the practical side, I would strongly encourage you to start your day reading the Bible. Establish a routine to get God's word into your mind and heart. Where should you begin? Well, if you have never regularly read the Bible, start with just a few minutes a day, every day. Ask the Lord what he'd like you to read, and ask him to help you understand what you are reading. I'd suggest beginning with verses that highlight the truth of your salvation. If it helps you, go back to chapter two and reread the verses I have discussed. Take some time to study these scriptures, and ask God to deepen your understanding of what Christ has done for you. Or, if you'd prefer, read through a book of the Bible, like the Gospel of John or the book of Romans. Consider reading just a chapter a day, prayerfully thinking about what you have read. You will find your soul being strengthened. With God's help, you will begin to understand in a deeper way Jesus' love for you. It will be well worth the time and the effort.

I try to begin each day by reading a chapter in the book of Proverbs, a Psalm, and at least a few verses in the New Testament. Today, for example, I read Proverbs chapter 28 (since it is June 28th), Psalm 58, and Revelations 3:8-13. I try to read carefully and prayerfully, asking God to encourage my soul and give me wisdom for the day. For me, the Bible is the main course of my spiritual breakfast. It is how God speaks to my soul. Reading scripture reminds me of who I am in Christ. It helps give me a biblical perspective of Margaret's illness. It reminds me of God's faithfulness and his love for me and my family. It stabilizes my soul to face the day with faith and confidence in the Lord.

Also, I try to keep scriptural truth fresh in my mind throughout the day. In the middle of life's busyness I can easily become spiritually drained. The reality of God's provision and care can seem distant, clouded in the pressures of my work responsibilities. So, in my desk I keep a set of verses. Some are printed, others are hand written. When I get a chance, I try to take a strategic break to refocus my heart on God's truth. As I pause to read these verses, I am reminded of his love for me. My soul is refreshed in the knowledge of who God is, and his precious promises for me. This brings a renewed sense of calm. The whirlwind of my multiple tasks is brought into a healthy Christ-centered perspective. I get a needed dose of God-given strength to face the tasks before me.

Margaret's Bible intake looks a bit different. With all her assorted health issues, it is very difficult for her to consistently read her Bible. So, as a part of our daily routine, each morning I read out loud to her. Currently I am reading from two different daily devotionals,

"Practical Encouragements"

both of which start with a scripture. These are *Look Unto Me, the Devotions of Charles Spurgeon*, edited by Jim Reimann, and *Diamonds in the Dust*, by Joni Eareckson Tada. As I read, I pray that the verses and the author's comments will strengthen and comfort her soul. Though some days it is hard for her to concentrate through her waves of pain and fatigue, the Lord has faithfully given her sufficient spiritual food to persevere. Even if she can only focus on a single verse or part of a verse, God has kept her faith and trust in him consistently strong. If you also find it difficult to focus due to your medical symptoms, be encouraged by these words penned by Margaret Clarkson:

> Suffering is seen as one of God's means of enlarging the soul's capacity for Himself, and sufferers are enjoined to seek God's enabling that they may lose none of the present or future fullness that God would have them experience as a result. . . . There is only one way in which a sufferer may come to realize the eternal good which is God's purpose for him in pain, and that is by a close study of the Word of God. Sufferers often find it difficult, even impossible, to maintain any systematic pattern of Bible study; but God in His mercy has not forgotten such needy ones. Scripture abounds with what I like to call God's fragments—a host of all-encompassing minutiae which, though fragmentary and seemingly unimportant in themselves, are nonetheless capable of nourishing and sustaining the seeking soul.[37]

As a closing thought on this topic, please take full advantage of your pastor's teaching ministry. Pay close attention to what he communicates in his Sunday messages. Take good notes, and during the week prayerfully read them over. Discuss the content of the teachings, and their application, with your family and church friends. Let God's word take deep root in your heart, and ask the Lord to "[transform you] by the renewal of your mind" (Romans 12:2). His desire is to use the teaching ministry of your church to provide your soul with an abundance of spiritual food. Feast on it, and watch him deepen your walk with the Savior.

Now it's time to look at the third aspect of my *Big Three*: Prayer. Simply stated, prayer is talking to God. Yet in our action-orientated, activity-driven culture, at times I have underestimated its importance. I have wondered, "Does prayer *really* make a difference?" After all, for years I have asked the Lord to heal Margaret, and her health has steadily gotten worse. If God is going to answer "No" to my biggest request, is it really worth the time to pray to him? Should I really take time out of each day to pour my heart out to the Lord, knowing that ultimately he is orchestrating everything according to his sovereign plan? Rather than praying, shouldn't I be doing things that are more tangible and productive? Well, what I have learned is, despite the mystery that attaches itself to prayer, prayer is vital. Getting alone and expressing my heart to the Lord cannot be ignored. If I want to get to know Jesus better, and see God's hand in our medical circumstances, I need to regularly pray. Ponder these words by Paul E. Miller:

"Practical Encouragements"

> Learning to pray doesn't offer us a less busy life; it offers us a less busy heart. In the midst of outer busyness we can develop an inner quiet. . . By spending time with our Father in prayer, we integrate our lives with his, and what he is doing in us. Our lives become more coherent. They feel calmer, more ordered, even in the midst of confusion and pressure.[38]

You see, if we desire intimacy with Christ, if we want our relationship with the Lord to grow, we must pray. If we want the assurance in our souls that he will be with us and help us through every aspect of our medical trials, we have to talk to him. It is so important "we integrate our lives with his." Every hurt, every moment of confusion, every need, should be shared with our heavenly Father. Remember "the eyes of the Lord are toward the righteous and his ears toward their cry" (Psalm 34:15). He carefully listens when we pray to him. We have his undivided attention, and he delights to spend time with us. His will is we experience his calming presence, no matter how intense our suffering may be.

The Lord wants to help us make prayer an integral part of our entire day. Over the years I have found myself talking to God more frequently and more honestly. During my day I breathe a lot of silent prayers, some simple and work-related like "God help me to teach this completing the square lesson," to more desperate pleas of "Lord, how to do expect me to have the strength to parent my teens, work full-time, and give Margaret the proper care? Please help me!" Sometimes I shout out my requests. Other times I feebly mumble the words. But I know he desires for me to "continue steadfastly in prayer, being watchful in it with thanksgiving" (Colossians 4:2). He doesn't tire of my voice. He wants me to realize, in an ever-growing way, that he is the One to run to first. When, by his grace, I do call out to him, I see his hand of provision. I experience peace and contentment. I have the joy of sharing my day with my Savior.

If prayer has not been a significant part of your life, I would encourage you to dwell on Psalm 62:8: "Trust in him at all times, O people; pour out your hearts before him; God is a refuge for us." The Lord wants you to pour out your heart to him. Maybe, due to the severity and longevity of your illness, all that wants to come out of your heart is anger and bitterness. My encouragement? Start there. Tell the Lord exactly how you feel about everything that has happened to you and your family. Get everything off your chest. Have a good, long heart to heart with the living God. It is the first step to deepening your relationship with him. He wants to hear from you. He longs for the communication lines to be reopened. For there, in his presence, you will begin to see freshly how he is your only true refuge. You will be positioned to sense his love, comfort and direction. Your prayers will extend well beyond the ceiling. They will be heard by the One who loves you, died for you, and is interceding for you (note Hebrews 7:25).

With God's help, aim to make prayer an important part of every day. Pray in private, pray at work, pray with other believers, pray whenever you sense the need. As a Christian, the Lord loves you as his child, and loves to spend time with you. I pray God will give you a renewed awareness of how much he cares for

"Practical Encouragements"

you, and how much he delights to spend time with you (If you'd like, feel free to go back to chapter four and reread the key reasons to pray.) During the long days of chronic disease and disability, may you experience his precious comfort and peace through times of prayer. He is the God who "comforts us in all our affliction" (2 Corinthians 1:4). He never grows weary in our communication with him. What a blessing it is to be able to have a living relationship with the living God!

In concluding this section, I pray the Lord will continue to help you to cultivate your relationship with him. May you experience his grace to grow in worship, Bible study, and prayer. May the Lord give you wisdom to put in place beneficial routines that enrich your faith, and your awareness of his love for you. May he also help you to pull any spiritual "weeds" in your life (things that you see are hindering your relationship with Christ) so that your Christian walk can be strong and fruitful. What a joy and privilege it is to have God's love and care through every aspect of our health challenges. What an honor it is to be able to share our deepest needs with our loving Lord.

Now let's proceed by looking at another practical encouragement: making every effort to strengthen your family. Yes, through his love and grace, your family can actually be strengthened during times of illness. By the transforming power of the gospel, you can apply biblical truth and experience God's miraculous power to persevere. How thankful I am for God's grace to help our family during our many years of disease and disability! I pray that what you are about to read will help your family as well.

Make Every Effort to Strengthen Your Family

We consider it a miracle of God that our family has been able to endure all these years of chronic disease. Because of his love for us, the Lord has given us the power to persevere. Despite over two decades permeated with medical trials, our family has not been driven apart. Sure, like any family, we have our times of conflict, and the stress of Margaret's illness can bring out the worst in us. But by God's grace, I can honestly say that our love as a couple, and the love we share with our children, is stronger than ever.

I attribute the preservation of our family to the Lord's love and care. Over the years he has faithfully provided for us, and has also guided us to keep our priorities in the right place. Sure, we have made mistakes along the way, and still make them. Yet his forgiveness and grace to keep protecting our family is a blessing we are very thankful for. So, here is a list of family-related practices that I would ask you to prayerfully consider. I hope these practical encouragements will help you and your family to successfully weather the storms of chronic disease.

#1: Make Your Marriage Relationship Your Top Priority:
One reality of long term illnesses and disabilities is that they will transform virtually every aspect of your life. Unpleasant symptoms and all that goes with them will penetrate even the simplest of routines. Everything from brushing your teeth to sitting at the dinner table together may take on a whole new look. If you are like me, with each of these transitions you will be tempted to murmur and complain. You will wonder why your

"Practical Encouragements"

family has to deal with this stuff, when so many other families don't have to. It won't be easy. You will need to pray much, and draw from the strength of the Lord.

Particularly in the marriage relationship, where the deepest levels of emotional and physical intimacy exist, illness can bring abrupt and unwelcomed change. If your spouse is the patient, the fusion of physical pain and new medications can result in intense and disheartening transformations. The person you love can be altered in both emotional and physical ways. Anger may suddenly fly out at you, and you wonder where his or her calm and caring demeanor has gone. As medications do their work, annoying side effects will likely enter the medical drama as well. Moodiness, weight gain, drowsiness, and a bunch of other undesirables could appear. The reality of new, crushing limitations could spur attitudes of ungratefulness, depression, or both. Most transitions in our lives are hard. Medical transitions are even harder, particularly in a marriage. Everything from holding hands while conversing to romantic times together can be permanently altered. Frankly, the whole marriage dynamic may be forever different from what a couple once enjoyed.

I can honestly tell you that everything I've shared in the previous paragraph has occurred to us (and quite a bit more). We have had to walk through some difficult seasons of change. These times have not been fun. The acceptance of medically-induced change is painful. It is all too easy to long for the "good old days," when things were more normal. Yes, our relationship looks significantly different than it did twenty-five years ago. Through the power of Christ, however, we have had the grace to make these adjustments. We are still together,

Always Sick, Always Loved

and share an intimate, committed relationship. The depth of our love for each other has grown over the years. With all the illness-related changes we have had to make, I can truthfully say to you that our relationship is better—different, but better. Better because God has been with us. Better because we have fought the medical battle as a team, and have experienced the comfort of the Lord as a team. Better because our loving Savior is passionate about the health of our marriage. Thank God for Jesus, and all he has done for us!

At this point I would like to give you a heart-felt plea: please do everything you can to protect your marriage. When physical or emotional changes occur in your spouse, seek the Lord. Make him your refuge. If the sexual aspect of your marriage is altered, be ready to resist temptation. Attractive, healthy members of the opposite sex will cross your path. Be on guard. Ask the Lord to help your thought life. Stay away from any relationship or situation that could undermine what God has given you with your spouse. "Flee youthful passions and pursue righteousness" (2 Timothy 2:21a). God's desire is your marriage grows through times of adversity. Your medical trial has *not* come into your life to destroy your marriage. Remember God is in control, he loves you, and will use the chronic illness for your good, and the good of your marriage.

A verse that has scared me in a good way over the years is Proverbs 6:32: "He who commits adultery lacks sense; he who does it destroys himself." Adultery has an inescapable consequence—self destruction. All Margaret and I share, all the love we have with each other and our children would be annihilated by this sin. This is why it is imperative to apply this verse: "Be

"Practical Encouragements"

sober-minded: be watchful. Your adversary the devil prowls around like a roaring lion, seeking someone to devour" (1 Peter 5:8). The enemy of your soul will send assaults against your marriage. Send an aggressive counteroffensive. Stay close to the Lord. Keep his word fresh in your mind. Surround yourself with godly friends who can encourage you. Frequently seek the Lord for strength and wisdom to build your relationship. Don't forget—"He who is in you is greater than he who is in the world" (1 John 4:4b).

The key scripture that has often inspired me in my care for Margaret is found in Ephesians 5:25a: "Husbands, love your wives, as Christ loved the church." As I have studied Christ's love for me and his church, I have been motivated to lay down my personal, self-centered desires in lieu of Margaret's needs. Christ died on the cross so that I could live. So too, on a daily basis (if not moment by moment) I should lovingly put aside what I want to do, and be ready to care for her.

Yes, a key foundation for every married couple, regardless of medical circumstances is this: *Love as Christ loves you*. Pause and let this sink in. How has Christ loved you? (Feel free to go back to chapter 2 if you need to.) He paid the ultimate price for your sins on the cross of Calvary. Despite the offense of your sins, he died so you might live. Through the Savior's atoning work, he has completely forgiven you. He rose again for your salvation. He is now seated in heaven, and "always lives to make intercession for [you]" (Hebrews 7:25). How vital it is to care for your spouse with the gospel clear in your mind. Prayerfully loving like Jesus will help your marriage relationship. Even with the all the complications that come with a disabling illness, God will build your marriage through the power of Christ.

The gospel is my example and my motivation to care for Margaret. Focusing on Jesus spurs me to sacrificially do all I can to help our marriage. Sure, my duties as a husband and caregiver are seldom convenient. And yes, sometimes I still bring her care with a lousy attitude. But Christ's example keeps me pressing forward. His love demonstrates to me over and over again that sacrifice is a good thing in God's eyes. Without Christ's sacrifice I couldn't be saved. Because of his death and resurrection my future is secure in heaven. So, it is worth it to put my selfish desires aside. It is beneficial to lay my life down in my care for her. Why? Because loving Margaret God's way brings life to our marriage. It deepens our relationship and yields added peace to our home. So, with this gospel-centered motivation in mind, here are some practical things that I would encourage you to consider.

First of all, spend quality time with your spouse. Give him or her your undivided attention. Turn off the TV, put your book down, look lovingly into his or her eyes, and let the communication begin. For us, some days Margaret is so ill, she is barely able to function, let alone have a quality talk with me. Nevertheless, it is still very important that I try to include her in my day, sharing with her my challenges, the decisions before us, and any new developments with the children. I also am continuing to learn to come to her eager to listen. Even if I am bursting to share something with her, I try to hear what's on her mind first. Some days what she really needs is my ear—not a lengthy discourse on what has been happening to me.

"Practical Encouragements"

Good communication brings security to Margaret. She sees that I want to talk to her. It affirms to her that I am not weary of her or her illness. You see, every so often Margaret will ask me, "Michael, do you ever get tired of the fact you are married to a sick wife? Do you ever wish you had a wife that was healthy, and could do more things with you and the children?" Despite my dogmatic "No's" to these questions, nothing says "I love you" to her like my companionship. Seeing I want to be with her speaks decibels louder than a hundred "I love yous." Frankly, this is no sacrifice for me. She is an incredible, beautiful lady, and for some mysterious reason, she loves me. Why wouldn't I want to spend time with her?

Secondly, be watchful for anything (even good things) that can weaken your marriage relationship. Except for your relationship to God, loving your wife or husband must be your top priority. Margaret is the one who should consistently see by my actions that my relationship to her is number one. When the kids were younger, she once shared with me how she didn't like the fact that I gave the kids their allowance before I gave her some spending money. That practice, though seemingly miniscule, left an impression with her. It made her feel like tending to the needs of the children was more important to me than she was. Particularly with all she deals with involving her illness, the visible message she gets from me must be loud and clear—I love her more than any other human being.

Along this same theme, I'd encourage you to monitor carefully your post-work activities. Be at home as much as you can. When my teaching day is complete, I try to get to our house as soon as possible. My being home is very affirming to her. It tells her that I cherish her, and want to be near her. This is why I have made adjustments to what I do recreationally. I try to make sure my times to unwind are nearby, and not too time consuming. Nowadays I prefer to visit a park in our neighborhood for a time of walking and light jogging. Sometimes my son joins me and we shoot hoops together. It is important Margaret knows I am readily available to her even if I am recreating. Relaxation for me does not equate to a lengthy time away from her—and this makes her feel more secure.

Also, all my supplemental employment is either done at home, or very close to home. When I have one-on-one math tutoring appointments, they come to our house. My part-time work as a manager at a retirement community is a mere three minute drive away. Summer school is done almost entirely online, allowing me to work from my home office. A couple of years ago, after completing my inaugural season as a basketball official, I decided to give it up. Why? Because as her illness has progressed, I know she needs me to be home more, not less. So traveling to gyms and officiating for three to four hours wasn't a good thing for us. I am learning that to love like Jesus means I must be near her as much as possible. When I am in the house she rests better, and she can see my love for her.

Thirdly, I would highly recommend keeping romance alive in your marriage. Aim for a consistent date time together. Plan private times for the two of you. Realize, however, that it may not be easy. Once again adjustments and special accommodations will need to be made. Particularly if your spouse is the patient, your dates are going to take on a new and

"Practical Encouragements"

unique look. Margaret and I used to like to go out to dinner and then catch a flick at the local movie theater. Now our date times are at home. Take-out food has replaced sitting in a restaurant. DVD's or TV movies are our theater of choice. Sometimes, if her sarcoid is flaring, she needs to sleep instead of spending intimate time with me. Our planned date time can quickly shift to an evening of rest and recovery. Despite the disappointment this can bring, I am continually learning how important it is to love her like Jesus—to be sensitive and flexible towards her in our chronic illness world. I know she still needs to see my affection for her. I pray the Lord will help me in the days ahead to continue to plan special, loving times that show my love for her.

In the realm of romance, I would also encourage spouses to be very understanding and considerate in your physical relationship. If your husband or wife is ill, or is the primary caregiver for a family member, please be very sensitive in your lovemaking times. Be careful to not let your desire for intimacy create feelings of guilt or pressure. There have been a number of times over the years when our expression of sexual love had to be put on hold. Though all was in place and the candles were lit, the intensification of Margaret's symptoms made it clear lovemaking would have to wait. Fatigue, pain, and breathing difficulties can be an intimacy killer. Many times holding the love of my life has had to be delayed. It is a reality of the chronic disease world.

How I respond during these intimacy postponements is crucial. What Margaret doesn't need to hear or see is a disappointed, complaining husband. What she needs is my reassurance that I love her, and am

Always Sick, Always Loved

willing to wait for the time she is able to physically show her love to me. Once again I have learned that a godly response can only come by the grace of God. As I focus my soul on Christ's love for me, I can put on hold my physical desires. What is most important is I love her unconditionally. I don't want her to feel condemned because she isn't able to hold me. Rather, I want Margaret to understand that I love her, and she is worth waiting for.

I would add here that it is very important to have open, honest conversations with your spouse about your physical relationship. It may feel a bit awkward, but talking about your sexual relationship will help each of you understand what modifications are necessary. As a disease progresses, the physical aspect of your marriage is going to change. Practices that were once fun and pleasurable can now be painful. So, mutual adjustments are going to need to be made. Again, look to Jesus. Prayerfully and humbly be considerate of what is best for your marriage. Though different, this new season of your sexual relationship can still be enjoyable and rewarding for both of you. I pray the Lord will help you to keep the fire of romance burning brightly even with the challenges of chronic disease.

In conclusion, I would like to reemphasize the importance of focusing on Christ's example of love. While reading the previous paragraphs you may have felt the sting of guilt for past or present failures in caring for your spouse. Maybe your spouse left you because he or she felt they could no longer endure the challenges of chronic disease, and longed to be free of the obstacles sickness brings. I have hopeful, good news. The Lord loves you. He desires for you to draw

"Practical Encouragements"

near to him. His forgiving arms are open wide to give rest to your soul and comfort in all your troubles.

Whatever pain you may be feeling in your heart right now, I would plead with you to come to Jesus. Share your deepest heartaches with him. Ask him to forgive you of your sins, and to give you a new, passionate commitment to him and to your spouse. If your marriage is wounded, God can heal the wounds. If your marriage vows have been broken, the Lord can show you a love even stronger than that between a husband and wife, his eternal love for you. Let's continue to rejoice in the reality expressed in 1 John 1:8-9: "If we say we have no sin, we deceive ourselves, and the truth is not in us. If we confess our sins, he is faithful and just to forgive us our sins and to cleanse us from all unrighteousness."

#2: Help Your Children to Have a Biblical Perspective:

When a disease or disability disrupts your family's world, the people who will probably need the most encouragement are your children. Sickness fires a consistent barrage of fearful messages at the heart of a child. They will need all the care and support you can give them to understand God loves your family, he is in control, and he will faithfully take care of all of you.

Our two children, Liz and Caleb, are now both teenagers (gee, I am feeling old.) Liz just graduated from high school this past May, and, in just a few weeks, Caleb is getting ready to begin his senior year. Looking back, living with a chronically ill mom has certainly affected seasons of their childhood. Seeing her battle a serious disease, and all that goes with it, is a path we would not have desired for them. Yet we know God

Always Sick, Always Loved

has allowed it according to his plan. Thankfully, despite all the difficulties over the years, we continue to be a close-knit family. To be sure, just like Margaret and I do, they have times of struggling to understand why their mom is sick, and why a loving God would allow her to continue to have such a challenging, sickness-filled life.

It is during their times of struggle that we have learned it is vital to have open communication with them. When Liz or Caleb asks a question, we try to honestly answer it. Not too long ago, while I was driving Caleb home from school, he asked me, "Dad, is Mom going to die?" Since Margaret was having one of her more difficult health weeks, the magnitude of her symptoms weighed on his teenage heart. I responded as straightforwardly as I could. "Son, I don't think she is going to die. I hope that day doesn't come for years. But, I have to trust the Lord with when Mom is going to die. For all of us, that day is in his hands."

I'm not sure how much comfort Caleb got from my words, but I tried to give him a truthful, biblically-based answer. Let's face it—children are very perceptive. They can usually tell when we are not telling them the whole story. So, in an age-appropriate way, we have always tried to tell our kids the facts, with an emphasis on the reality that God loves us, and he is in control.

But like anything that goes with the adventure of parenting, our example speaks infinitely louder than our words (I will be discussing this more in just a few paragraphs.) I hope Caleb had the affirmation in the car that afternoon that I was truly trusting God with the course of Margaret's illness. I don't just want to give our children the right scriptural answers. I pray, despite

"Practical Encouragements"

my sinful tendencies, that they see in my life what I am encouraging them to do.

So, my first encouragement to you would be to have age-appropriate, open and honest communication with your children. Allow them a context to freely share all their questions and concerns. If your child says, (as ours have) "I don't like God anymore—I have asked him to heal Mom for years and he never has—I refuse to talk to him anymore," don't overreact and respond with some heavy-duty corrective discourse. Rather, share how you have had similar feelings and thoughts. Express to them how the Lord has helped you. Use the opportunity to try to explain what gives you hope each day. Emphasize to your child the gratitude you have in your heart for God's love through Christ and the promise of his continual care. Let them talk to you about anything and everything—then gently point them to the One who can bring them comfort and peace.

Secondly, I would encourage you to carefully choose the activities your children participate in. Just like in a marriage relationship, time together as a family is crucial. It is very important that your children are not so overloaded with sports and other extra-curricular commitments that all of you are seldom home at the same time. Quality family time cannot just be scheduled. Beneficial communication can't just be a part of a day slotted on a daily planner. Families need to be together enough so that burdens can be shared. As best you can, make sure you are all home at least a few times each week.

When Caleb was in the fifth grade, his soccer coach enthusiastically expressed to me Caleb's athletic potential. He told me with top notch coaching and training my eleven-year-old could one day play soccer on a national level. To realize that goal, however, Caleb needed to start playing competitive soccer *now*. No more rec-league stuff for him. It was time for him (and us) to take the necessary steps to position Caleb to maximize his soccer skills.

I appreciated the coach's passion and desire for Caleb. But as I looked at the time commitment required for him to play competitive soccer, it became very evident that our family dynamic would be significantly changed. Practices during the week and tournaments out of town on weekends would greatly limit the time we'd have together. When I presented the competitive scenario to Margaret, she immediately expressed her concerns about how much time Caleb and I would need to be away. What she didn't want to see was our family weakened by absenteeism. Playing soccer in this context just didn't seem right to her—and I agreed.

So, as much as I loved seeing Caleb score goals, and as honored as we were to hear his coach's kind words, we decided to pass on competitive soccer. (It also didn't hurt that Caleb's real athletic passion is basketball—he didn't want to dedicate that much of his young life to soccer either.) Yet even if Caleb's favorite sport was soccer, we would have been hard-pressed to let him play. Caring for our family had to take precedence over athletic potential. For us, the competitive sports world just wasn't worth it.

Don't get me wrong, I think it is great to have our kids playing sports. Liz has played on a number of volleyball teams, and also ran track. Caleb plays basketball both in the summer and the winter. Athletic pursuits

"Practical Encouragements"

for them have been fun and beneficial. My point here is to be careful about the time that is designated for extracurricular things. Whether it is sports, music, or hobbies, keep your family first. Make sure you will still be able to have quality time together. Face your chronic illness challenges as a team, doing your best to guard the precious relationships you enjoy.

Thirdly, realize the power of your example. Be a role model for what you believe. This to me is a humbling thing, because I know how often I have sinned over the years in full view of Liz and Caleb. I have had to apologize to them often for my failures and sins. But despite my weaknesses, the Lord desires to show them the reality of my faith. He wants me to live before them the life-changing truth that believing in Christ is the key for living. Jesus is the reason we have been able to endure all these years of illness. He is our only true hope. It is actually good for them (and me) to have to repent for my shortcomings. It shows them I am not perfect, and I struggle just like they do. In a very personal way it also demonstrates to them once again that God's remedy for sin is forgiveness through the atoning work of Jesus.

I pray I can consistently show them who Jesus is by the way I live. I want my children to see me continuing to mature in my relationship with God. I desire for Liz and Caleb to observe how a biblical perspective of chronic disease brings stability to our souls. I trust our marriage, strengthened by the goodness of the Lord, will make a godly impression on their lives. By God's grace, as they understand more of what Christ has done for us, I pray many more open conversations will take place. We look forward to listening to more

Always Sick, Always Loved

of their burdens, frustrations, and concerns. We long for more quality time together. In the months ahead I pray the Lord will reveal to each of them how God is our refuge and strength in times of trouble.

Yes, Margaret and I strive to frequently share with Liz and Caleb all God has done for our family over the years. We try to keep before them the precious truth that we are experiencing the miracle of perseverance. Despite the longevity of her illness, we are still together. The love in our marriage is strong. Our family is tight in love for each other. This is a miracle from the Lord. How we thank God for his love for us!

#3: Keep Humor Alive in your Home:

Let's face it—there are a lot of gloomy things which tag along with a chronic disease or disability. Pain, sleep deprivation, medical bills, doctor's appointments, and a scary prognosis are just a few of the depressing things we may have to deal with. Serious circumstances stare at us each and every day. So, I think it is time to talk about some merriment. Despite all the non-fun things in your medical world, consider time for some light and trite. I think you'll find laughter is a healthy practice that will encourage your family.

To set the tone, I'd like to share with you one of the most embarrassing events of my life. As you'll see, laughter defused the situation. Instead of being humiliated, I was encouraged to laugh it off. Smiles and playful kidding made all the difference for me. My personal intensity was lightened by appropriate humor. Hopefully this real-life drama will encourage you to use humor in a healthy way. I trust you will be motivated to break your medical tension with an occasional comic

"Practical Encouragements"

moment. I pray you can still have some playful times together, even when circumstances are hard. Try not to have each day swallowed up in seriousness. A laugh and a smile can go a long way—check out what happened to me in the summer of 1988.

It all began when my dad invited me to join him and a few friends for a time of fishing on Lake Ontario. Our objective was lake trout, and our angling mission was to begin at dawn on Saturday. My plan was to rendezvous with my fishing companions late Friday night, catch a few hours of sleep at our rented lakeside cabin, and then rise with them about 4:00 a.m. If all went as planned, I hoped to be hooking some large fish well before noon.

The weekend excursion began on schedule. I left my apartment around 9:30 p.m. Friday, and arrived at the cabin a bit before midnight. All looked as I expected: the cabin's back porch light was on, and my dad's gold minivan was parked nearby. So, I quietly entered through the porch door, (my fellow fishermen were already asleep) helped myself to a glass of milk, and began to get ready for bed. I peeked into my bedroom (it was where I had slept on our previous visit) and I was glad to find it was neatly arranged and ready for my arrival. Wearily I crawled into bed, and quickly went off to sleep.

Around 2:30 a.m. I began to suspect something was awry. The two other bedrooms, just feet away from me, emitted sounds that were eerily unfamiliar. A heavy cough, strange mumbling, and non-Robble snoring made me a bit uncomfortable. For a few minutes I wondered who these raspy cabin companions were. But I concluded that Dad had probably invited a few more folks to join us—this had happened on previous fishing outings. Plus, my desire for sleep superseded any late night curiosity. I figured in the morning all would make perfect sense; and, it did.

At 4:30 a.m. the cabin was rattled by steady, loud pounding at the front door. In seconds I went from being out cold in dreamland to wide awake. As I lay on my bed wondering what was going on, one of my cabin mates walked heavily in the direction of the front door. He was clearly agitated, and in his gravelly voice said a few things that would give this chapter an R-rating. I heard him open the door. Then came my moment of revelation—the reason for all the strange noises of the night was about to be revealed. I heard my dad's voice, *outside*, apologetically saying these words: "Sorry to disturb you. . . But by any chance did my son come in here last night by *mistake*?"

The word "mistake" catapulted me up onto the edge of my bed. Then dogmatically my mystery cabin companion responded to my father's inquiry. "No, no one came in here last night." It was time to make my move. Sweat forming, I abruptly stuck my head out of my room and declared, "I'll be right there." Shocked, the man I had never met stood frozen as I rushed past him into the cool morning air. Did I really just spend the night with people I had never seen before? You better believe I did.

I was stunned, embarrassed, and perplexed as to how this had all taken place. Didn't I review the specifics with my dad beforehand? Weren't all the accommodations supposed to be the same as our previous trip? What happened?

"Practical Encouragements"

For my father, however, there was no need for an investigation into the error of my ways. This was his ultimate opportunity for humor. He took out his video camera, and with gut-shaking laughter he asked me to provide an explanation for the future viewing audience. With his camera zooming in on my shocked face, the questions began: "Mike, what just occurred? What did it feel like to illegally stay in a cabin? Why did you sleep in the cabin, when we were in the camper next door?" His laughter and playful kidding went on for hours. In fact, even years later he'd flash a grin and remind me of this infamous night on the shore of Lake Ontario.

Dad's response illustrates the blessing of a sense of humor. He could have greeted me with a stern rebuke about all the bad things that could have happened (later, I found out the other men in the cabin were police officers—that did freak me out a bit.) Instead, he defused the tension of the situation with playful kidding. He thought my mistake was hilarious and a family memory for the ages. So, rather than exiting the front door facing corrective criticism, I stepped into high decibel laughter.

Sometimes it is good to laugh. It is healthy to take an exit from all the seriousness in our lives to smile. It is beneficial to try to not make everything doom and gloom. In an appropriate way, I'd recommend we all try to laugh once in a while. In the Robble family, despite the seriousness of Margaret's disease, we still try to find some comic relief.

There is a wonderful verse in the book of Proverbs that states, "A joyful heart is good medicine, but a crushed spirit dries up the bones" (Proverbs 17:22).

I apply this scripture in my own life by first seeking to experience the joy of the Lord. I ask God to help me focus on Christ and all he has done for me. I thank the Lord for my salvation, and the promise of his love and care. Pointing my soul at Jesus gives me joy. This joy is not based on our circumstances, but on God's promises through Christ. This is real joy—and I thank God for it.

I also look to apply this verse by trying to keep humor in our home. Being joyful, happy, upbeat, is "good medicine." Merriness and laughter does help diffuse the weighty atmosphere of chronic disease. This doesn't mean I make light of Margaret's illness. Rather, in an appropriate way, I aim to keep comedy alive in our illness-filled world.

Sometimes I employ self-deprecating humor. I poke fun at myself. I tell Margaret the reason she has lung issues is because she is married to me. After seeing me in a bathing suit on our honeymoon, I took her breath away—and it has lasted a lifetime. This is why we consider our life love song to be the classic, *Take My Breath Away*. I inform Caleb not be discouraged after his workout at the fitness center. Pointing at my feeble right bicep, I tell him, "Don't worry son. It took me years of training to chisel my arm like it is today. There is still time for you." Yes, my strange Robble humor is a fairly constant theme in our household. Sometimes the family reminds me my jokes aren't funny—that's OK, because I am having some fun trying.

We also use TV and movies to bring in some comic moments. Old sitcoms we watched in our younger days (like the *Cosby Show*) can generate smiles on even the most depressing of days. *Princess Bride* (our all time favorite movie) is a regular on our entertainment agenda. As a family we sit together and watch some good, old-fashioned comedy. These times have been a welcome change of pace for us as a family. Yes, laughter and sickness can be in the same room together. It is healthy for your family. Let yourself unwind despite the challenges of illness. Try not to take your life and medical circumstances too seriously. Don't let the strain of chronic disease keep your home from times of laughter.

I trust what I have just shared encourages you to strengthen your family. With God's help, may you experience a deeper love for each other despite the hardships that come with illness and disability. Now, let's look at another important practical encouragement, which is so crucial in every chronic illness situation: care for the caregiver. I pray what I am about to share helps you like it has helped me.

<u>Care for the Caregiver</u>

On a crisp December evening in 2006, I received a phone call that would forever change my direction as a caregiver. On the line was my sister Sue, who lives in the small town of Remsen, NY. "Susan Dear" as I fondly call her, (she calls me "Michael Dear"—don't ask me why, it's one of those long-standing Robble-isms) had decided it was time to have a heart to heart conversation with me. After her traditional greeting of "Michael Dear, how are you?" she efficiently got down to business.

Her mission was clear. This was no call about the latest family news. Susan's agenda this night was to push me to take a long look at myself. Compassionately she began the interrogation. "Mike, when was the last

Always Sick, Always Loved

time you got a physical? " "Uh, I don't know, a few years ago, I guess," I mumbled. "When was the last time you saw a dentist?" My insides started to squirm. "When I broke a tooth a few years ago, I think." Her parade of planned questions continued. "How often do you exercise? Are you eating right? Do you get enough sleep?" I barely had time to conjure up my answers. The more she had to say, the more it dawned on me that I hadn't been thinking much about my well-being. She wrapped up her verbal barrage with a passionate exhortation: "You know, if you come out the other side of Margaret's health struggles sick yourself, what is going to happen to your family? Caleb and Liz need you. You can't crash and burn because you are wearing yourself out to care for Margaret. Please don't forget to take care of yourself!"

Within minutes after we concluded our conversation, the importance of what she said began to weigh on me. As Margaret's primary caregiver, I had been living with an attitude of invincibility. I figured the Lord would protect me even if I foolishly pushed myself again and again past the point of exhaustion. At the time of my sister's call I felt physically OK, and assumed I would continue to be graced with strength for all that needed to be done. Hey, Margaret needed my care, and as her husband I was the primary person to give that care. My focus was to expend all my energy, each and every day, to make sure her and the children had everything they needed. My daily agenda was permeated with this driving focus: work, work, and more work. I didn't think taking time to care for myself was all that important.

"Practical Encouragements"

As I prayed about this, I sensed God's conviction. I felt the Lord reminding me that I was only a man, and I had the same limitations as anyone else. It was prideful to think that I could continue to push myself like I had been doing. If I persisted in this pattern of self-neglect, some type of breakdown was inevitable. Sue's phone call was my wake up call. I was being warned through my sister that now was the time to start making wiser personal choices. Yes, every health scenario has two patients: the person with the illness, and the primary caregiver. Margaret has a regimen of medical care designed by her doctors. I too, as her caregiver, needed a personal treatment plan as well.

Note these provoking thoughts from medical provider Kaiser Permanente (you'd think "Susan Dear" read these just before she picked up the phone to call me):

> Taking care of yourself is your most important step as a caregiver. Caregivers are more likely than those who are not caregivers to be at risk for colds and the flu and also chronic illness, such as heart disease, diabetes, and cancer. On the other hand, when caregivers take time to care for themselves, good things usually happen: They stay healthier. They feel better about themselves. They have more energy and enthusiasm and can keep giving care. Here are some important things that you need to find time to do-just for yourself: Get some exercise. You may feel better and sleep better if you exercise. . . Eat healthy meals and snacks. . . Get enough sleep. . . Make time for an activity you

enjoy. . . Get regular medical checkups. This includes dental checkups. Even if you have always been healthy, you need to stay healthy.[39]

With these thoughts in mind, I'd like to share with you what I have done over the past few years to better care for myself. It started with making an appointment for a complete physical. If you are a caregiver, I would suggest making this your first step as well. Have your health thoroughly checked out. Get the blood work done. Don't hide anything. Be totally honest with your doctor. Let him know of any symptoms you have been having. Listen to his recommendations.

It had been a few years since my last physical. When I saw my doctor early in 2007, the test results and exam gave me some clear medical direction. As my physician evaluated my health, our first conversation was about exercise—or, should I say, my lack of exercise. I had gained some weight in the years since my last physical. Also, my blood tests showed a high level of bad cholesterol. Since heart disease runs in my family, he told me I needed to develop an exercise routine. His suggestion was brisk walking around thirty minutes a day, five days per week. He also suggested I gradually turn the walking into light jogging. The thought of walking or jogging didn't appeal to me. Thirty minutes five days a week also didn't stir my enthusiasm. I naturally don't like to exercise. It is work, not fun for me. But I knew if I was going to take better care of myself, I needed to start regularly working out.

What followed was the culinary lecture. My high cholesterol needed to be managed by changing how I ate. Exercise would help, but dietary adjustments were

"Practical Encouragements"

also pivotal. What he said didn't surprise me: less fatty foods, more fruits and vegetables. I needed to be more diligent to eat healthier. No more coming home from work and downing large quantities of potato chips with a tall glass of cola. For my well-being, I needed to be more selective with the foods I consumed.

When I told Margaret my medical results and the doctor's recommendations, she pleaded with me to be diligent to follow through. In a loving way, she began to police my health. She did her best to make sure I ate healthier—more fresh fruits and vegetables, fewer fatty foods. She kindly ordered me to begin exercising. I started with walking, and gradually progressed to a combo of walking and jogging. Neither she nor the children wanted me to become ill while I was caring for them. I was now on their medical radar, and their support has helped me to take better care of myself.

Though I still need to be more consistent with my diet and exercise, I am grateful for the benefits I have seen over the past few years. Today I am happy to report my bad cholesterol is back in the normal range. I have been able to lose some weight. I have added energy and deeper sleep than I used to have. My feelings of stress and "being in knots" have been helped by exercising. I thank God for helping me to take better care of myself.

The next phase of my personal care came by seeing the dentist. After my physical I made an appointment for a dental evaluation. I had always tried to make sure Margaret and the children were on track with their dental checkups. Yet I had not been routinely seeing a dentist for years. In fact, it had been over ten years since I had seen a hygienist for a cleaning. Sure I

Always Sick, Always Loved

brushed and flossed every day, but over that decade I felt no urgency to interrupt my schedule by coming to a dentist's office. My only visits were for emergencies, like a broken tooth or a lost filling.

When I did have my oral examination, my dentist told me the only reason that I didn't have more severe gum disease was because I flossed. I don't know the exact poundage of tartar in my mouth, but the pictures he showed me were quite gross. As we were discussing how my teeth would be cleaned, my hygienist reminded me that heart disease and other illnesses are more likely to occur in people who neglect their dental hygiene. I took her message to heart. Over the next two months a couple of extensive appointments were scheduled. With the support of mouth-numbing injections and a nuclear-like cleaning tool, all the tartar was blasted off my teeth. When the process was done, boy, did my teeth feel great. I had to come in every three months for about a year to make sure my gum disease was in check. Now today, with everything up-to-date, I am grateful to report my mouth is healthy.

To summarize, having an annual physical and regular dental check-ups have become a normal part of my life. Exercise, eating better, and sleep is my personal trilogy of health habits I try to monitor closely. Sure, some weeks go by and I am not as diligent as I should be. But since my sister's call I now have a deeper understanding of how important it is to care for the caregiver. I have even thrown into the mix a few vitamins and naps: on the vitamin front, after breakfast I take a supplement for men over fifty and 2000 mg of vitamin C. As far as naps go, if my nighttime sleep is poor, I aim for a brief "power" nap in the late afternoon. Yes, thank

"Practical Encouragements"

God, it has sunk in that I need to take care of myself, so I can better care for those I love.

Now let's continue the journey of practical encouragements by focusing on how you can be a blessing to others. Ready for a friendly challenge? Take it, and I think you'll be pleasantly surprised at what the Lord will do through you.

Look to Encourage Others— Take the 15 Minute Challenge

Despite my years of experience seeing the faithfulness of God, I confess by September of 2011 I had slid deeply into my own private pit of despair. Margaret's first hospitalization of 2011 (she was admitted in June) saw her swelling in all her extremities, with the complication of fluid building up in her lungs. At first her physician thought the cause of these symptoms was heart failure. Hearing these words broke me. I trembled and sobbed. Was the Lord now going to take my lovely wife, just as our youngest child was getting ready to start high school?

Thankfully, after a few days it was determined her condition was caused by a drug interaction. A couple of her medications had blended their side effects together to yield the life-threatening symptoms. Margaret was prescribed IV diuretics, and in about a week her body came back to normal. I was so grateful the Lord had given the doctors wisdom, and I was praising God when the day came that I could bring her home. With the hospital stay now behind us, Margaret slowly started to regain some strength, and I was able to resume my working routine of teaching summer school.

Always Sick, Always Loved

Just a few weeks later, however, our world was medically shaken again. Onslaught #2 was more intense, and more crippling in nature. It started with ever-increasing lower back pain. Then inflamed feet joined the fury. It was like the perfect storm of physical discomfort—two horrible fronts of pain combining to make her as miserable as possible. This hurricane of pain got so bad that Margaret could only sit on the edge of our bed and moan. She was almost out of her mind in pain. She couldn't bear to move, let alone try to walk. I called 911. After a brief evaluation, the paramedics knew she had to go to the hospital. So, in less than a month, she was back getting treatment for a severe medical condition. I wondered. . . "God, what is going on?"

After several hours in the emergency room she was admitted for observation and further tests. A day or two later she was diagnosed with strained back muscles and gout. Her back had been injured during a session of in-home physical therapy. Her gout was triggered by stomach flu-induced dehydration. Thankfully her pain levels subsided after a few days, and she was given the green light to come home. Weakened physically and drained emotionally, we once again drove out of the hospital parking lot. I was discouraged. "Lord," I pleaded, "Could we have a restful end to our summer? Please?"

So much for wishful thinking—in mid-August came hospitalization #3. Unbearable stomach pain and nausea prompted another call to 911. The paramedics again lifted her up, placed her on a stretcher, and carried her out of our home. Another ambulance ride—more hours in the emergency room—yet another hospital admission. This time it was determined she needed

"Practical Encouragements"

to have her gall bladder removed. Surgery came, followed by a few days of recovery. Once again she was released, and for the third time we were driving home depleted by medical troubles. What a summer. What an exhausting sequence of physical suffering.

Looking back, I regret that during this time I allowed myself to get more and more isolated. The catalyst of my solitude was my anger at God. I felt we had suffered enough. I *really* didn't get how all these hospitalizations were a part of his good plan for us. It was so hard to see Margaret keep suffering like this. I just felt like I couldn't take anymore. So, I gave the Lord the silent treatment; and as a result, I didn't want much Christian interaction either. I drifted into a mode of spiritual hibernation. I just wanted everybody to leave me alone, and give me some time to figure this out. I began to like my pit of despair, where people left me alone to ponder how hard our summer had been.

I chose to stay home more, missing Sunday services and Wednesday's small group meetings on a regular basis. Sure, on some of those days Margaret really needed me to be home to care for her. Yet at other times I figured I deserved the rest. I wasn't plotting to blatantly forsake the Lord after our summer of strain. I just thought I'd quietly distance myself for awhile as I tried to recover from our numerous medical monsoons.

But, thank God, along the way the Lord used our church to help me out of my pit of despair. It was during hospitalization #3, when a spiritual seed was planted by our pastor Glynn McKenzie. After visiting with Margaret and me in her hospital room, Glynn offered to buy me dinner at the hospital sub shop. As we were consuming our six inch sandwiches, he said this to me: "Mike, I know Margaret's illness gives you a lot of challenges, and can be very consuming, but I don't think the Lord wants her illness to define you. It is going to be a big part of your life, but it shouldn't consume your life. I believe there are plenty of people who could really benefit from what God has allowed you to experience. Ask the Lord to help you to live above your circumstances, and be used to bless other people."

At first I wondered about the sanity of his thoughts. Could God really use us to bless others? Throughout the summer I felt like I was on an episode of Christian *Survivor*. I wanted to do the right things so I wouldn't get kicked off God-Pleasing Island. Yet I preferred to survive the onslaught with minimal human contact. Others were not supposed to join me in my pit of despair. So, with all our medical turmoil, why should I take time for others?

Well, in the days that followed, Glynn's comments gave me a measure of spiritual nutrition that far exceeded the benefits of my tasty Italian sub with whole grain chips. It was a fresh reminder that God didn't want me to just focus on us. Sure, my plate was quite full with everything from doctor's appointments to further medical tests to taking my teens to the mall. But as I prayed about what he said, this verse came to mind: "Let each of you look not only to his own interests, but also to the interests of others" (Philippians 2:4). Was the Lord showing me a means to lift my head out of my depressing, hibernating pit of despair? *Yes!* It was by setting aside time each week to try to bless others.

To show how individualistic and self-absorbed I had become, I felt like the Lord simply put on my

"Practical Encouragements"

heart to aim to give just fifteen minutes per week to someone else. It was like a personal challenge of commitment. "Mike, can you give fifteen minutes this week to encourage a person you know is suffering?" Fifteen minutes? Of course I could give fifteen minutes. Gee, can I sacrifice the last half of *Sports Center* to pray for or call a person in need? Sure. Yet the truth was for the months surrounding our hospital triathlon I rarely gave anyone outside of my family fifteen minutes a year, let alone fifteen minutes a week.

So, with God's help, here is what I did. I first prayed, and asked the Lord who could use some encouragement. I asked God to show me who was feeling alone in their struggles, and could use someone to talk to. As folks came to mind, I reviewed their names with Margaret. She would focus on praying for and reaching out to the ladies. I would direct my time towards the men. It might be a medical trial, a financial trial, or a variety of other trials. Regardless of the type of suffering, the goal was to encourage these people by simply reaching out to them.

So, my fifteen minute challenge began. It started with a phone call to Aaron, a man in our church who had been struggling with chronic back pain. We talked. We laughed together. I had the joy of praying for him. Now, months after that first phone call, I am privileged to say he is a close friend. In fact, Aaron even took me up on an invitation to watch me officiate. He got some free entertainment observing me run up and down the floor, being verbally peppered by fans. I received the joy of his fellowship as we enjoyed a cool beverage at a coffee shop right after the game.

Thankfully fifteen minutes a week has just been the beginning. I have also been getting to know other men as well, both in and outside of our church family. I now try to take some time almost each day to pray for or reach out to someone who is hurting. Without a doubt the encouragement has flowed both ways. I am grateful they have appreciated my friendship, and I have been enriched by their friendship as well.

For me, the fruit of reaching out to others has been significant. I have been reminded of God's faithfulness and love for his people. Hearing what the Lord is doing in the lives of others has given me timely encouragement. It has helped me to understand the futility of giving God the silent treatment. Whether times are easy or hard, he is at work in me, and in my church family. My personal relationship with Christ has been enriched by getting to know my brothers and sisters. Though I sinfully withdrew from those who cared about me the most, the Lord has lovingly deepened my relationships with my friends in Christ.

So, in the theme of practical encouragements, I would strongly suggest making a regular part of your life reaching out to others. Start by just making a phone call. Pray for them. Follow up a few days later. Get together with them. What God has done for you, can in turn encourage others. And, like me, you will also be encouraged. Take the fifteen minute challenge, and watch the Lord multiply it for his glory, and for the good of his people.

As I conclude this chapter, I pray you have been strengthened and challenged to make wise practical choices for you and your family. I have tried to discuss what I believe are the most important things you

"Practical Encouragements"

can do to help you and your family endure a serious medical condition. May the Lord help us to make wise decisions that strengthen our faith, our family, and ourselves so we can persevere for the glory of God.

Discussion Questions

1) Describe your current involvement in a local church. If you belong to a local church, what can you do to deepen your relationships with your fellow believers? If you are not part of a local church, what is your plan to find a church family?
2) How has the medical situation you are facing affected your family? What, with God's help, do you hope to change or put in place to strengthen your family?
3) Who is the primary caregiver in your home? What can you do to help him or her be better cared for?

Margaret's Reflections

On a brisk, January afternoon, our friend Jamie Frampton came to our home to interview Margaret. Despite the challenges of her ongoing symptoms, Margaret was able to spend a couple of hours with Jamie, and share with her about her life with a chronic illness. What you are about to read are the highlights of their conversation, which we call "Margaret's Reflections." I hope the spontaneity and openness of their time together will minister to your soul.

Always Sick, Always Loved

Jamie: How does your knowledge of the gospel affect your daily life?

Margaret: When I first wake up Michael reads two different devotionals to me. One by Joni Eareckson Tada and another by Charles Spurgeon. That always starts my heart in the right direction in the morning. The years that I was able to memorize scripture have benefitted me now too. If I start to get depressed or feeling "woe is me" then those scriptures are there before I get very far in that thought process. I make the choice to have my thoughts go in a different direction. It used to be a lot more depressing when I would go for months and years not making it to church. The isolation factor can affect my focus for the day. But people in our care group and church have grown in serving me by visiting regularly. They are wonderful; they come along and we can talk about the Lord or watch a movie or both.

Jamie: Are there particular parts of the suffering you experience every day that make it hard to value what the Lord has done for you?

Margaret: Some days focusing on what the Lord has done is hard; sometimes because it just doesn't enter my mind because the pain is so intense. There is no comparison, however, with what Jesus went through on the cross. I shut my mouth when I think about the things they whipped him with, the experience of having his skin shred, of all he went through for my salvation.

Jamie: When has the knowledge of God's love helped through an experience?

Margaret: One of the most difficult times was a two or three month period when they thought I had cancer.

"Practical Encouragements"

This was before I got the diagnosis of sarcoid. I was in the hospital for several days at this point. I felt like I had already received a death sentence. But then the night nurse came in while I was sitting on the side of the bed. She wrapped her arms around me and told me she would be praying for me. That is how the Lord works: through people. People have communicated God's love for me and that knowledge has strengthened me in the midst of trials. Friends have come and visited me in the middle of the night, and no matter where you are, your pain is more intense in the middle of the night. One year, I was on bed rest during Christmas and a friend flew out to do Christmas shopping and cook hot meals for the kids. I didn't even get to see the Christmas tree that year, but felt encouraged by how people cared for us. Our friends who live in Arizona sent a big care basket with restaurant gift certificates and movies for me to watch. Even though it was depressing, the thoughtfulness of people showed me that the Lord was still blessing me.

Before Christmas I was angry because I couldn't do anything to help or participate. Caleb came over to me and leaned down by the rocking chair I was sitting in and said "Mom, I know you know this but you've got to remember that the important thing about Christmas is Jesus and not presents or cooking." Though I didn't say it out loud, I thought in my head "oh shut up," but those types of negative incidents in my head I can count on one hand. That is just a gift from the Lord that I haven't had a harder time with depression.

Jamie: Is it a struggle to feel refreshed in your walk because you've suffered for so long with the same trial?

Margaret: Well, the struggle is changing because it's always getting worse!

Jamie: What are some practical things you've found to be helpful in developing your relationship with God?

Margaret: When the disease blossomed, the children were still being home schooled. At that time, Caleb would read me a few chapters of the Psalms. Now I enjoy reading Christian novels and personal testimonies that are inspiring. Listening to things online has also been helpful.

Jamie: Do you struggle feeling condemned because of your suffering or thinking that God is punishing you?

Margaret: I struggled with this more the first couple of years I was sick. I was pretty much cast aside because people believed I was trying to get attention. In the early years I wondered why God was beating me up and what I did wrong. For a long time now, I haven't felt this way. After being dragged over the coals a few times because people expressed what they thought was wrong with my life, I finally learned to guard my heart and stop listening. I think I wonder more now why God is letting me suffer. Or I want to know why I can't just go home to be with the Lord.

Jamie: Does the thought of heaven occur to you frequently?

Margaret: All the time, especially when the pain is flaring up really badly. I used to think that in a trite way, but now it is different when I think about how I am doing, I don't want to say things that are offensive to the Lord. I don't want to just say things because that is how I am feeling. Sometimes when I think about leaving here, I catalog my life and wonder what I've

"Practical Encouragements"

really done. I think of Joni Eareckson Tada and just feel like I haven't done anything.

Jamie: Is watching your kids experience your illness hard?

Margaret: That is the worst part of it. The knowledge that anything can happen is hard. Each child handles it differently. Some people have said that it was wrong for us to adopt when I was sick. But you can't protect your family; there is so much we don't have control over. My father had a much different reaction to suffering. He was deaf from the time I was 3 and he considered that his deafness was a lifelong curse. He could also find a lot of negativity in things because his mind wasn't always on the Lord.

The kids have struggled because they have both been praying for my healing since they were able to pray and when nothing changed, they concluded that prayer doesn't work. Though it might sound light, trite, and glib, the truth is that sometimes God says no. He doesn't give us everything we think we want; he gives us what we need. But it is hard to make sense of things like that. But we have no promises of a trouble free life and despite the illness, we need to look for the blessings. Our family is still together, our marriage is still strong, we have a roof over our heads. We have to focus on what God has done for us rather than what we don't have. With sarcoidosis, you feel like you have cancer and you'll struggle with the same level of pain, but it doesn't ever kill you. I want my children to know that I fought to stay with them and I didn't give up.

Jamie: Has your understanding of who God really is changed your experience of suffering?

Always Sick, Always Loved

Margaret: I felt guilty for the longest time because when I first got sick we were in a church that believed that sickness and suffering were sin. I was told that I was holding Michael back and keeping him from being a church leader. It has been a gift of God that I haven't struggled with depression. I don't really have to fight to stay happy, that is a gift from God. The joy is truly from the Lord. I don't really think about it too much. I don't dwell upon my trial, I think about what I'm going to cook for dinner that night.

Jamie: Is prayer something that you can participate in easily or is it hard because of the illness?

Margaret: Because I am at home alone most of the time, I don't find prayer to be a routine as much as a part of daily life. I have the house to myself and find myself talking out loud to God much of the day. Reading is much harder for me to concentrate on. Michael reads to me, which is really helpful and starts the day right. Prayer is more of a conversation. I have found it to be ineffective to rebuke the Lord, so I've learned to have more reverent conversations with Him. A friend of mine told me the Lord was telling her to encourage me that I have a unique time at home, while unable to move a lot, to be praying for others and making the most of my time that way. If I feel like I'm not doing well remembering to pray, that word always comes to mind. It is hard to pray when I haven't slept and I can't think clearly.

Jamie: If there was something you could communicate to people who have never experienced chronic suffering, what would you want them to know?

Margaret: I think it was Spurgeon who said everyone needs to have a good month of illness. I might add onto

"Practical Encouragements"

that not being able to breathe or walk or vomiting at the dinner table and other things that are just embarrassing are things people should pray to understand. I worked at a hospital for 15 years and I cringe now at the way I treated people. It isn't that I was insensitive, I just didn't get it. And less is more. Don't tell people that you know they are going to get better, just offer to pray for them and admit that you don't have a clue what they are going through. Don't try to relate your bout of the flu with their lifetime illness. Truly you don't get it unless you've lived it. But if you live long enough, it is coming. No one gets an exemption.

Jamie: What has helped you to be more content?

Margaret: I haven't really ever come to that point where I just completely gave up. It isn't very often that I wrestle with contentment. That is another work of God.

Jamie: How have you experienced being part of a church even though you can't attend because you are home bound?

Margaret: I've had many friends come and visit me in the hospital. It has been such a relief to not be alone all the time. Many times I've said I don't know how people with chronic disease can make it without a church family. So many friends faithfully commit to visit, sometimes bringing dinner, sometimes bringing a movie to watch. Friends who have come just enjoy my company and have blessed me. I don't always want people to come over with the perspective that they are here to serve me and see how I am feeling; I appreciate friendships and good conversation. Even something as simple as someone listening to me and remembering that I mentioned I like spinach tortilla dip and bringing it over or knowing what my kids like to eat means so much. Our care group took up a donation once to get me a new walker because my insurance company wouldn't cover a new one. Friends came over Christmas day and delivered it.

I pray someday you will have the opportunity to sit down and have a conversation with Margaret. She'd love to meet you, and have a chance to hear about what the Lord has done for you. But if you never get to meet her here, as a believer, one day you will have the opportunity to see her in heaven. For through Christ we have hope—not only for this life, but for all of eternity. Now let's turn our attention to that blessed hope, found only through our Savior Jesus Christ.

Chapter Seven

"Eternal Hope"

> "And not only the creation, but we ourselves, who have the firstfruits of the Spirit, groan inwardly as we wait eagerly for adoption as sons, the redemption of our bodies. For in this hope we were saved. Now hope that is seen is not hope. For who hopes for what he sees? But if we hope for what we do not see, we wait for it with patience" (Romans 8:23-25).

Our culture is fascinated with predictions and forecasts. Turn on the TV, read a newspaper or magazine, surf the internet, and soon you will find a prediction of some sort. They permeate virtually all aspects of today's media. Here are just a few I have come across recently: Today's weather is sunny with a 10% chance of an isolated afternoon thunderstorm. For the next quarter, the national unemployment rate is anticipated to be 8.1%. The total debt for student loans is expected to reach $10,000,000,000 over the

Always Sick, Always Loved

next decade. Trends, anticipated growth or decline, who could be the next president, these and an abundance of other topics find their way into the land of forecasting.

Forecasts and predictions also give our culture a sense of hope and direction. Optimism or doom and gloom can hinge on a projected trend or event. Typically the more likely something is to occur, the more confident we are to plan a course of action linked to that event. Remember Y2K? Many experts anticipated the grid would go down when the clock struck midnight on January 1st, 2000. This meant for hours (or possibly days) public utilities, such as electricity and water, could be rendered inoperable. I made the mistake of going to a grocery store the afternoon of December 31st, 1999. I was swallowed in a sea of humanity loading up on cases of water and batteries. The apocalyptic-like predictions had propelled people into survivor mode. As things played out, a number of folks had long-lasting supplies of H_2O and flashlight batteries that year. The projected grid collapse never happened.

The type of predictions I enjoy the most involve professional sports teams. I find it interesting to see how the designated experts of sports are able to determine which teams will be winners and which are destined for a year of competitive futility. One of my favorite reads involves Major League Baseball. Every year *Sports Illustrated* produces their MLB season preview issue, where a baseball superstar gets to adorn the cover. In the pages that follow, their skilled writers describe everything from who will be the top hitters and pitchers to which teams are ready to make the playoffs. They look at trends, who is due to have a

"Eternal Hope"

"break out" year, and which players are most likely to fade on the baseball horizon. Statistics are analyzed, diligently digested, and other intangibles are factored in. Thanks to their efforts, I can get some inside information on how our Colorado Rockies and other teams will fare this coming year.

I got a sport's "kick" a few years ago while I was in the waiting room at a doctor's office. With a bit of time on my hands, I scanned the office magazine racks in search of some relaxing reading material. What I found was the 2010 *Sports Illustrated* baseball preview issue. What made this fun was the 2010 baseball season was already over. Empowered by my after-season knowledge, I decided to take a look and see how accurate the writers were. Had they picked the division champions? Were the top hitters and pitchers for 2010 those they had selected? After reading for just a few minutes, it was clear in a number of instances they were off. Injuries had decimated some of the teams predicted to do well. Shining rookie performances had stirred other teams, forecasted to be basement dwellers, into the playoff hunt. Other players had dream seasons, playing at a much higher level than they ever had before. The baseball experts had given it their best shot—they just couldn't anticipate all the variables that affect and define a team's season. I wondered how many fans had their hopes stirred after reading the author's predications. . . only to be crushed weeks later when all he wrote became more fiction than reality.

In the arena of chronic disease and disability, we have our own "preview issue" of sorts. In fact we have two preview issues. One is based on what we can see, and one is based on what we cannot see. Here is the first one—it is what paints a sad picture before us every day. It targets our illness, our disability, our hardship, and where it all is leading. This, to be sure, is the depressing forecast. It is confirmed over and over again in the stadium called real-life. Optimism does not flow from these projections. This look to the future tells us we are all destined to physically wear out and break down. The frailty and mortality of our human frame will catch up to us. Everyone ages. Everyone suffers. Eventually everyone dies. In most cases our chronically ill loved one will never get any better, and in fact will progressively grow worse. These trends are a sure thing; they have played out over and over throughout human history. Everyone's health "preview issue" projects a loss of mobility, and an increase of disabling affliction—not exactly a heart-inspiring read.

If we live long enough, the fate of our bodies is certain. Psalm 90:10 drives home our mortality: "The years of our life are seventy, or even by reason of strength eighty; yet their span is but toil and trouble; they are soon gone, and we fly away." Sure, we might make it into our eighties, but by then our bodies will have endured just about all they can—and at a moment determined by God, we will die. As the scriptures say, "it is appointed for man to die once, and after that comes the judgment" (Hebrews 9:27).

Feeling encouraged? Probably not. A human medical preview is not an enjoyable, relaxing read. So, how can I call this chapter "Eternal Hope?" If we are all destined to face disease, disability and death, what is there to hope for?

Well, here is the good news: there is a second "preview issue." This edition is not based on what we can

"Eternal Hope"

see. In fact it is so glorious that it is even beyond our ability to accurately imagine. Yes, "what no eye has seen, nor ear heard, nor heart of man imagined, [is] what God has prepared for those who love him" (1 Corinthians 2:9). Thank God, there is a guaranteed future for the Christian. And this future, which continues for all of eternity, is a 100% without-a-doubt promise. How do I know this? I know this because it is based on the true, inspired words of scripture. It is anchored in the Person of Jesus Christ. Praise God, the perspective of our lives isn't intended to be based on what we see. Even with nagging pain and disability, we can have hope because of who Christ is. He has been faithful to us in the past. He promises to take care of us in the present. He will be with us through everything that is coming in the future. Truly he is our hope. Therefore we do not need to be afraid—no matter how medically serious all may appear to be.

The focus of this chapter is on the wondrous, eternal hope we have in Jesus. God's "preview issue" is one that will strengthen your soul and inspire you to face every season of your chronic disease knowing that the Lord will be with you. I would like to frame this chapter by first discussing some inspiring highlights from the 23rd Psalm. This passage of scripture emphasizes the Lord's continual, never-ending care. Then I would like to look back, and share with you some of the special blessings we have experienced as a direct result of Margaret's illness. I pray as I remember the Lord's faithfulness to us in the past it will encourage you as well. Finally, I would like to conclude by discussing the glorious reality of heaven: the home of the Christian for all of eternity.

Always Sick, Always Loved

Hope from Psalm 23

Of all the passages of scripture that have comforted and inspired me over the years, my favorite is the 23rd Psalm. I think what I enjoy the most about it is its applicability to every season of life. Particularly during the most difficult times of Margaret's illness, this set of verses has reminded me time and again of the Lord's never-ending love and faithfulness. So, in a concise way, I'd like to share with you the key soul-strengthening truths of this Psalm. Before I begin, I want you to know that I owe much to what I have gleaned from these verses to W. Phillip Keller. His book, *A Shepherd Looks at Psalm 23*, has helped me immensely to understand and apply these scriptures. So, as we look at this wonderful Psalm, I pray the Lord will minister to you. Let's start by reading Psalm 23:

> The Lord is my shepherd; I shall not want. He makes me lie down in green pastures. He leads me beside still waters. He restores my soul. He leads me in paths of righteousness for his name's sake. Even though I walk through the valley of the shadow of death, I will fear no evil, for you are with me; your rod and your staff, they comfort me. You prepare a table before me in the presence of my enemies; you anoint my head with oil; my cup overflows. Surely goodness and mercy shall follow me all the days of my life, and I shall dwell in the house of the Lord forever.

"Eternal Hope"

As we start to dig into these verses, keep in mind what Jesus said in John 10:11-12: "I am the good shepherd. The good shepherd lays down his life for his sheep." So, it is imperative we study this Psalm through the lens of the atoning work of Christ. For the Christian, Jesus is your good Shepherd. On the cross he gave his life for you. Since he has saved you, you are now one of his precious sheep. So, read this passage as a revelation of Jesus' heart for you. His love is so deep and far-reaching that it can seem too good to be true—but it is true. So, take these verses very personally—because they are all about God's heart of love and care for you, his child.

So, let's begin. "The Lord is my shepherd; I shall not want." Do you see the personal nature of this verse? The Lord is *my* shepherd. That's right; the Lord (the almighty Creator of the universe, who came to earth and died for your sins) is *your* shepherd. These verses are about *your* Savior. Every word here applies to *you*. If you are a Christian, no matter how beaten down you may feel right now, every promise in this Psalm is for *you*.

Let the word "my" in the first verse grip your soul. If need be, say out loud right now, "the Lord is *my* shepherd." This reality is amazing and true. The eternal God is forever fused to you. He will always take care of you. He will never change his mind about you. What does this mean? You are never alone. You will always be protected and provided for. You will forever be lovingly nurtured in every part of your life's journey.

So, since God is your shepherd, you "shall not want." All your needs will be taken care of. Your Savior knows and understands every detail of your medical struggle. He is aware of your every need: spiritual, emotional, physical, and material. What an inspiration this is to pray! The Lord wants to intimately provide for all your needs. That is his heart for you. Make him your refuge, and come to him boldly in prayer. Your will be blessed when you see his faithful, abundant provision.

Ready for some more inspiration? "He makes me lie down in green pastures." Sheep only can rest when they know they are safe. Fear of predators, annoying insects, and a host of other irritations will keep a sheep on his feet. Yet, when a flock knows their shepherd is nearby, when they are continually well-cared for, it is easy for them to lie down and rest. So too it is for the child of God. Knowing Jesus is ever near, trusting in his provision and care, enables the Christian to rest. Thank God, because of the faithfulness of Jesus, we can have rest in our souls. We can have God's peace, no matter what our circumstances. Yes, as a Christian, the Lord will help you to lie down in a pasture of assuring rest.

Next, "he leads me beside still waters." Sheep often get their greatest intake of water when eating grass covered by the morning dew. This supply of moisture, hanging still on the blades of grass, can provide enough water to sustain a sheep for hours. This is a picture of God's heart to peacefully fuel us daily with his presence. Particularly in the early morning, when we need our spiritual strength renewed to face the day, he will water our souls. What a blessing it is to know the Lord's heart for us! Every day he knows what our soul needs—and he promises to bring us soul satisfying, spiritual refreshment.

Feeling way past the point of exhaustion? Are you so weary as a patient or caregiver that you just want

"Eternal Hope"

to quit? Be strengthened through this promise: "He restores my soul." In his book, Keller discusses what happens when a sheep is "cast down." He describes it like this: "A cast sheep is a very pathetic sight. Lying on its back, its feet in the air, it flays away frantically struggling to stand up, without success... If the owner does not arrive at the scene within a reasonably short time, the sheep will die."[40] Have you ever felt this way? I know I have. With all the crushing difficulties of Margaret's illness, there have been a number of times I not only was knocked down, but I also didn't believe I had the strength to stand up again. There I was, down on the circumstantial canvas, hopeless to rise unless God intervened.

Thankfully the Lord did intervene (and continues to intervene). He gave me strength when I had no strength. He injected my heart with hope when all looked hopeless. He brought a supernatural restoration to my soul. How grateful I am for this promise: "he restores my soul." Are you currently feeling "cast down?" God wants to help get you back on your spiritual feet. Cry out to him. Claim this promise. Jesus is the great soul restorer. He knows exactly what you need to persevere in the marathon of chronic disease.

Note as well how the Lord guides us. "He leads me in paths of righteousness for his name's sake." Sheep cannot lead themselves. If a shepherd were to ignore his flock and let them go wherever they desired, danger, malnourishment, sickness, and death would soon follow. So too, the Lord knows we need his direction and leading. Life is just too hard and complicated for us to figure out what to do on our own. So, our loving Shepherd promises to lead us for "his name's

Always Sick, Always Loved

sake." Did you catch that? It doesn't say he is going to lead us where we necessarily want to go. He is going to direct us to where *he* wants us to go. A shepherd is fully aware of what is best for his sheep. He knows the goal of the journey. Every twist, turn, and detour is designed to get his flock to the best grazing land. We, as God's children, also need to remind ourselves that Jesus knows exactly what the best path is for us. He wants to bring us into a richer relationship with him. Christ is the perfect Shepherd. So, we can completely trust him to guide our lives.

Also, when life is at its most difficult, we don't need to be afraid. "Even though I walk through the valley of the shadow of death, I will fear no evil, for you are with me." Often to get to the best grazing lands, a shepherd has to take his flock through narrow, treacherous valleys. In a valley there is less sunlight, and limited paths to travel on. Danger can be the greatest, since predators can easily hide in the clefts overlooking the valley below. In our lives there are also those times that are more dark and treacherous. The Lord can seem far away, hidden by the multitude of troubles that bombard us in our deep places of medical despair.

Yet no matter how dark or deep the valley, the Lord promises to be with us. Even if death should come—God assures the believer he will never be alone. Historically, my greatest fear has always been Margaret's death. Though I know her passing would bring her into the presence of Christ (I will discuss heaven a little later in this chapter), I was terrified about what would happen to us. Particularly as I thought about how Liz, Caleb, and I would pick up the pieces of our shattered lives, dread and anxiety gripped my soul.

"Eternal Hope"

Then about a year-and-a-half ago the Lord did something very special for me. He gave me peace about our medical future, even if it did lead to Margaret's death. This assurance from God came to me after I prayed with our pastor about my fears. I knew the Lord wanted me to be prepared, in his strength, to face the possibility of watching Margaret die. Though I had no idea whether her departure was going to be soon or far off, I knew the Lord didn't want me living in fear. Since that precious time of prayer, the words "I will fear no evil, for you are with me" have strengthened me a number of times.

The truth is, we do not need to be afraid, even in the darkest times of our lives. Our troubles will never be so severe that they supersede the Lord's ability to care for us. God will never abandon us in our times of greatest need. On the contrary, he promises to never leave us or forsake us. The words "you are with me" is the message of greatest comfort. Jesus not only understands and promises to care for us. He promises to always to be with us, even during the most shattering events of our lives. I'd like to conclude my discussion of this verse by hearing again from Phillip Keller. Here is his description of God's care when his wife was dying of cancer:

> I was keenly aware of [his] consolation when my wife went to "higher ground." For two years we had walked through the dark valley of death watching her beautiful body being destroyed by cancer. As death approached I sat by her bed, her hand in mine. Gently we "passed" through the valley of death. Both of us were

quietly aware of Christ's presence. There was no fear—*just a going on to higher ground. . .* During my wife's sickness and after her death I could not get over the strength, solace, and serene outlook imparted to me virtually hour after hour by the presence of God's gracious Spirit Himself.[41]

There is also great encouragement found in this reality: "your rod and your staff, they comfort me." The rod speaks of a hard wood pole that was used by a shepherd to ward off predators. It was also used to keep the sheep on course. If a sheep started to wander away from the flock, the shepherd would hurl his rod near the sheep to scare it back to where it should be. The use of the rod was vital for the sheep's protection and care.

Thank God, these same principles apply to us. We are always in his sight. No matter how complex the medical trouble, Jesus is committed to protecting our souls. He does not let us wander away from him for long without getting our attention. If we begin to live in a way that is harmful for us, he will bring us needed correction. At times I have felt the sting of God's rod. Reaping the consequences for my own sin, the Lord has corrected me and put me back on his path of righteousness. I am grateful for these times of correction, for they have brought me closer to Jesus. What a blessing it is to know of the Lord's protection and correction! What great love Christ has for us!

Our Shepherd also has a staff. The staff was the tool of the shepherd, lighter and narrower than the rod, which had a hook-shape on one end. The main purpose of the staff was to gently grab or "hook" the sheep and bring them closer to the shepherd. Particularly lambs, who needed to be close to their mothers, were often moved by the shepherd using his staff. How this illustrates the Lord's desire for us to be close to him! How often Jesus gently woos us back to himself. Our living Lord desires that we have an intimate relationship with him. As our Shepherd, he wants us to walk close to him through every stage of our lives.

I hope you are being encouraged. I know I am as I reflect on these truths afresh. Let's continue our journey in the 23rd Psalm: "You prepare a table before me in the presence of my enemies." Before bringing his sheep to higher ground, a shepherd would typically go on a scouting mission. He would take great care to thoroughly inspect the grazing land of the high plateau. The word "table" was often used to describe these rich, higher elevation locations. It was imperative he went ahead of his sheep to insure these lands were safe and beneficial for the sheep. Sometimes poisonous plants were growing alongside the nutritious foliage of the plateau. These deadly plants had to be removed before the sheep arrived. Wild animals also might be in the area, and the shepherd needed to know where they lived and how numerous they were. Watering locations were another necessity that had to be located and prepared. The shepherd's diligence in inspecting these higher grazing lands secured the sheep's safety.

Do you see the application for the Christian? God goes before us. He makes sure all is prepared according to his plan. Nothing surprises him, for he knows exactly what is next in our journey. As Jesus said, "he goes before them, and the sheep follow him, for they know his voice" (John 10:4). What a comfort it is to know the Lord knows what is coming in our lives. Our illness-filled path has been completely checked out by our Savior. So, we again have no reason to fear. We can follow the Lord with confidence. We can be assured the Lord completely understands all we are going through. He has already prepared our "table" and will protect us from the enemy of our souls.

The provisional blessings continue: "You anoint my head with oil; my cup overflows." Good shepherds were always on the lookout for insects or diseases that would irritate the head of a sheep. It was crucial a sheep's head was protected from anything that could lead to more serious problems. So the shepherd, particularly in the summer, would often apply an oily mixture to the sheep's head. This was a slimy insect repellent and medicinal treatment that comforted and protected the sheep. Pesky bugs and skin diseases were no match against this thick, oily fortress.

So too, as God's children, the Lord wants to anoint our minds with his barrier of protection. He wants us thinking right—seeing the physical suffering in our lives with a Christ-centered, biblical perspective. By his grace, we can "be renewed in the spirit of [our] minds" (Ephesians 4:23). This makes all the difference in how we perceive our sickness and disability. A God-focused mind won't easily succumb to the irritating thoughts of condemnation, bitterness, and despair. Biblical thinking leads to godly living. Through the loving care of Christ, chronically ill people can have frequent thoughts of gratitude and thankfulness. They can love Jesus passionately because their minds are more fixed on his goodness than the pain and inconvenience they have

"Eternal Hope"

to live with. Thank God, Jesus anoints our heads during our medical battles. May we continue to think rightly and live in a way that pleases him.

And no wonder that we now see these words: "my cup overflows." With such an amazing, loving Shepherd, how can we not be a grateful people? The cup of our hearts should truly overflow with thankfulness. As I reflect on our life with chronic disease, sure, there have been a number of really rough times. Yet as I write this paragraph my heart is full of gratitude for all the Lord has done and continues to do for us. Despite my failures, he has been my faithful Savior. He has always been with us. He has always sustained us. He has enabled us to persevere. Thank God for the loving provision of Christ Jesus! Our cup overflows!

Now we come to the closing thoughts of the 23rd Psalm: "Surely goodness and mercy shall follow me all the days of my life, and I shall dwell in the house of the Lord forever." Let me try to capsulate it this way: for all our days on this earth, God will always take care of us. For every stage of a disease or disability he will be there. He will give our souls comfort. He will show his goodness. When we sin, he will extend forgiving, compassionate mercy. Our God, our Shepherd, is with us for the long haul. And as believers, when we do finally go through the valley of death, he will be right there with us as well. In fact, we will dwell in his house, heaven, for all of eternity. What hope comes through this Psalm! What a great comfort it is to know Jesus is our Lord, Savior, and Shepherd!

Another means to find hope is to remember what the Lord has done for you. The memory of God's provision and care can build your faith. It can remind your

Always Sick, Always Loved

soul of his faithfulness. So, I'd like to reminisce with you for a little while. I'd like to share with you some of the greatest blessings we have received because of Margaret's illness. Join me now as I travel down Robble memory lane—I pray hearing of our blessings in the past will strengthen you now and in the future.

Hope From Remembering

The old saying goes, "Hindsight is 20-20." The inference of this simple saying is that when we look back, we can usually see things a lot more clearly. What once was a cloudy, confusing storm in our lives with time can be seen as a precious gift of experience. Days of intense suffering can become visible as crucial seasons of growth. If we live long enough, we can begin to get a glimpse of how everything does fit together for our good.

To be sure, as I discussed in chapter three, we can never fully see the entire purpose of what God has allowed in our lives. His ways are above our ways, and it is impossible for our finite minds to completely understand the mysterious "whys" of what has come our way. Yet looking back at what the Lord has done can give us fresh hope in our current challenges. It can strengthen us to face the future. Some visible fruit from our illness journey can remind our souls that God is in control, and he is truly guiding our lives according to his plan.

King David exclaimed, "Remember the wondrous works he has done, his miracles and the judgments he uttered" (1 Chronicles 16:12). In the spirit of this verse I would like to recollect with you some of the blessings we have seen as a direct result of Margaret's illness. As you will see, I have organized these highlights into four categories. For brevity's sake I have tried to be selective, and I pray what I share will encourage you in the Lord.

Here is the first blessing I'd like to mention: *Knowing God Better.* In Philippians 3:10, the Apostle Paul said "That I may *know him* and the power of his resurrection, and may share in his sufferings, becoming like him in his death." Our medical adventure has had many ups and downs. We have endured a host of diverse symptoms and real-life health dramas. We have suffered, agonized, and cried. Yet we have not been alone. Jesus has been right there with us, pouring into our souls his divine comfort. Seeing his comfort and care has deepened our knowledge of who God is. We have come to understand in a very personal way his heart of compassion for the chronically ill. To me this has been the greatest treasure of all our years of health troubles: knowing the Savior better.

Through all the seasons of Margaret's pain, through all the times when I have been exhausted and spent, through all the hours of desperate prayer, God has revealed to me more about who he is. He has shown his love and care for our family time and time again. How do I know Christ understands our struggles? How have I been able to write the things I have in this book about the love of the Savior? Because the deep valleys caused by chronic disease have pressed me into seeking and knowing Jesus in a more intimate way.

How I thank God, that despite the times I have angrily distanced myself from him, he has always faithfully brought me back to himself. He has taught me he is our only true refuge. Instead of growing in bitterness and resentment, I have grown in appreciation of the love of the Savior. Margaret's illness has been used to change my life forever—by deepening my personal relationship with God.

This is why it is so important, as Christians, to tell our souls that hardship isn't a bad thing. An easy life is not a better life. I don't wish trouble on anyone, but the biblical reality is that God uses pain to mature us. Let's face it: without exhaustion, we wouldn't experience his supernatural strength. Without great needs, we would never see his great provision. Without weeping, we would never know his comfort. Yes, all the years of Margaret's illness have been immeasurably beneficial. Why? Because the Lord is more real to us today than ever before. By his grace we have been able to get to know him better.

I would encourage you to keep seeking God as your refuge. As you do, he will continue to help you progress in your understanding of who he is. You will see his strength and provision. You will become more and more amazed at Christ's incredible gift of salvation, and his personal love for you. Yes, as suffering pushes us to our knees, it also causes us to understand where our true help comes from. And as we seek his help, we get to know our wonderful Lord and Savior more.

Now let's look at my choice for blessing number two: *Deepening of Relationships*. In watching HBO's series *Band of Brothers*, I was moved by seeing the dedication and determination of the men from Easy Company. From boot camp to D-Day and beyond, these World War 2 soldiers trained, fought, bled, and some died together. Often embarking on very dangerous

"Eternal Hope"

missions, the soldiers united to fight against the oppression of Nazi forces. The fruit of all they experienced together in war-ravaged Europe created a relational fusion of their hearts. They would be forever a band of brothers. Facing death, guarding and supporting each other in the heat of battle, yielded a lifetime cementing of these men. It was a bond that went way beyond the scope of normal human relationships.

In our battle with chronic disease, we also have seen a precious deepening of relationships, starting with our family. Through the years of facing the onslaught of Margaret's sarcoidosis, we have learned to love and appreciate each other more. Liz, Caleb, Margaret, and I have had to rally together against a common foe. Sarcoid has thrust us into a medical battle. Our front lines involve everything from household chores to Margaret's medical care. As a unified team, we have had to roll up our sleeves and share the load. In the process we have learned to watch out for each other, and be more sensitive to each other's needs.

Margaret's illness has also built deep channels of open communication. As a family we typically are able to talk about everything and anything. Sure, sometimes sinful attitudes flow in our conversations. Shouting and anger may invade a discussion—but we talk. Little is held in. Apologies may be necessary after frustrations are vented, but our teens know that they can come to us and share their hearts. How is it that we share so openly? It is because over the years Margaret's illness has made us discuss some heavy-duty stuff. Our family communication lines have had to be open. This has created an atmosphere of freedom to express ourselves that I thank God for.

Honestly, we love it when our kids share their lives with us. One example of this was when I was teaching both of them how to drive. The months of our teens having simultaneous learner's permits did age me a bit. These were not relaxing moments in the car for me. Most of the time, from my instructor's position in the passenger seat, I said things like: "Slow down," or "Watch for the car in your blind spot," or "Brake a little sooner next time." Yet when Liz or Caleb was behind the wheel, I seldom heard anything driving-related. Both would open up to me about their goals, dreams, and hurts. While I nervously watched them turn right on red, they made sure I was in the loop on the upcoming events in their lives. I am so grateful we can talk to each other. I am so thankful the bridges of communication have been developed through the years of our family's challenges with chronic disease.

I would also like to add here that Margaret's illness has also been a catalyst in deepening our relationships with others. As I mentioned in chapter six, particularly those who have come alongside us in our suffering have become dear friends. There is a cherished group of folks in Arizona, and here in Colorado, with whom we share a special bond. They are the ones who have demonstrated God's love to us during our most trying times. They have prayed for us and blessed us in a multitude of ways. These friendships didn't just happen. They were nurtured over years of love, prayers and practical help during our seasons of suffering.

Now let's move on to blessing number three: *Seeing God's Provision*. There is so much I can write here. In order to keep this section from becoming too long, I'd like to choose just a few special highlights of

"Eternal Hope"

the Lord's provision. I'd like to start with how the Lord gave me a job in 1991.

As you may recall from chapter one, early in 1991 Margaret and I took a trip with her parents to Arizona. This was our month-long medical reconnaissance mission; we had to know if the desert climate would bring relief to Margaret's chest pain and breathing issues. With the almost instantaneous relief she experienced, the question of moving to Arizona was a no-brainer. The *huge* question to me was how to find a job in a state so far away. Our rural New York apartment was some 2300 miles from Phoenix. I also had only five years of full-time teaching experience. Combine the geography with my limited resume' and we had our own version of *Mission Impossible*. Would schools even ask me to fly in for interviews? If so, would this require a New York to Arizona commute multiple times?

As I initiated my job search, I hung a state map of Arizona on the bedroom wall of our apartment. Then I took a permanent maker and drew a thick line across the middle of the map. The location of Phoenix showed me how low the line could go. This would be my future employment reference line. Any school district on or below the line would be an acceptable potential employer. My goal was to land a job in southern Arizona—where continuous warm (or hot) weather ensured Margaret the most respiratory relief. With this horizontal line giving me geographic guidance, I began the time-consuming process of sending a cover letter and resume' to every school district in the southern half of the state.

In the weeks that followed I got little to no response from my inquiries. One day I did receive a letter from

Always Sick, Always Loved

a school district near Tombstone, Arizona. Remember Tombstone? It was the site of the famous shootout at the OK Corral. I excitedly opened the envelope to see if this would be my first request for an interview. Not quite. . . They sent me a requisition form for school supplies. Someone had mistakenly thought I was in need of crayons, wide-ruled notebook paper, or some other educational necessities. No, they didn't need a math teacher. There would be no algebra classes for me in the vicinity of this historic western town.

As May of 1991 rolled around, I found myself discouraged. It was clear to us that we were supposed to move. The New York climate continued to beat up Margaret, with chilly spring rains bringing searing pain to her chest and lungs. Yet without a job to go to, I couldn't just head out to Arizona. I needed to see God's green light: a teaching job near the Valley of the Sun.

Then one day in early June our phone rang about 4:00 p.m. The baritone-voiced man on the line introduced himself, and informed me he was the principal of Cactus Shadows High School. I was momentarily stunned when he told me Cactus Shadows High was in Cave Creek, Arizona, just a few miles north of Phoenix. I was even more dumbfounded when he told me he was looking for a full-time math teacher—and he thought I might fit the bill. Then he proceeded to tell me he saw no need for me to fly to Phoenix for an interview (that floored me even further). Rather, he asked if we could set up a phone interview. Within a couple of days I was on a conference call, fielding a bunch of teaching-related questions from the principal and the head of the Cactus Shadows math department. The next day the principal called me back. His words were few, but

"Eternal Hope"

carried immense significance for us: "Mike, welcome to Cactus Shadows High School. You are hired."

I had gotten the job, without ever meeting in person anyone whom I would be working with. In fact, the principal who hired me over the phone was long gone by the time I got to Cactus Shadows. He accepted a new position at a different school weeks before we moved—I never met the man. We rejoiced in God's incredible provision, and started finalizing the details of our move. Yes, the light was green for us to move to the desert!

There is one other amazing example of God's provision that I feel I must share with you. It involved our two trips to the Mayo Clinic in 2007. Having just dealt with the humiliation of bankruptcy, the last thing I wanted to see was us re-entering the deep, dark world of medical debt. So, before our trip to the clinic I called our health insurance company multiple times. I wanted to be "triply" sure our medical coverage would pay for most of the costs we were about to accrue. At the conclusion of each of these calls, our health care provider assured me the bulk of all the medical tests and appointments would be covered. In fact, I was told our projected maximum out-of-pocket cost would be about $3000. Considering the severity of Margaret's symptoms at that time, to me it was a worthwhile investment. After all, she was severely disabled from the aftermath of her prednisone treatment, and I feared she was going to die.

Throughout our two trips to Mayo nothing came my way to cause me to question the $3000 estimate. Each visit to the clinic had pretty much gone according to plan, and we were grateful for the medical counsel we had received. So, when I got an itemized statement from Mayo Clinic a few weeks later, I anticipated seeing a bill in the $2000 to $3000 range. When I opened the envelope I was shocked by the numbers staring at me. We owed them $13,685.18! I trembled. I almost cried. How could I possibly pay this?

As the dust settled on my not-so-God-honoring reaction, I first assumed this must be a mistake—a clerical error of some kind. Yet after further inquiry with their billing department, it was evident the mistake was on me. Our health insurance provider had a different payment scale for medical costs than Mayo Clinic did. Somehow I had missed this detail during my previous phone conversations. I did owe Mayo Clinic over $13,000!

So, what could we do? Well, thankfully, first we prayed. We asked the Lord to show us what we should do. A day or two later Margaret's sister Nancy called and encouraged us to talk to Mayo about their financial assistance program. So the next day I was on the phone with a lady in their Patient Account Services office. I didn't mince words with her. I nervously told her of the shock of seeing such a large, unanticipated bill. I informed her we were still reeling from our recent bankruptcy. I also let her know on my salary I saw no way we could pay this bill in a timely manner. She then asked me a few questions about our family, my income, and the severity of Margaret's illness. I very much appreciated her kind and compassionate tone. I knew she would go to bat for us financially. I just wasn't very optimistic that much could be done.

She concluded our conversation by asking me if I could fill out some financial assistance paperwork. She

"Eternal Hope"

explained to me that over the years a number of folks had donated money to the Mayo Clinic to help people in our kind of circumstances. She went on to say that typically the people who made donations put some specific criteria on the use of their funds. For example, the money may have to be used to help pay for specific tests, or only go to a family with small children. So, she felt our chances were slim of getting significant financial aid; but she felt it was definitely worth a try.

There was no news on our request for weeks. I assumed my next communication from Mayo Clinic would probably be to finalize a payment plan. Oh me of little faith. I never dreamed that the Lord would bless us in the way he was about to. You see, on a sunny October afternoon my world was about to be rocked— shaken by God's hand of provision.

I was driving home from work when my cell phone rang. Seeing the unfamiliar number with an Arizona area code told me this was probably Mayo Clinic calling. As I steered our car into the left turn lane at 112th Avenue (yes, I do remember where I was when I got the news), I answered the call. It was the lady with whom I had talked to in Account Services. She simply said this: "Mr. Robble, I just want you to know that your account balance at Mayo Clinic has been adjusted from $13,685.18 to zero. You will be receiving a letter in the mail communicating this adjustment as well." My vision began to blur from happy tears. My voice began to crack, quivering due to the magnitude of what I had just heard. I asked her to repeat what she just said; I had to be sure I wasn't audibly hallucinating. She affirmed, "Your balance has been adjusted from $13,685.18 to zero."

God had used the generosity of others to pay our debt in full. The letter confirming our financial miracle came in the mail a week later. I still have it, as a reminder of the Lord's love and compassion towards us. Yes, in the darkest of hours, God hears our prayers and can bless us beyond our wildest dreams. He doesn't give us more trouble than we can bear. How I thank him for the Mayo Clinic miracle!

There are many other examples which come to mind when I reflect on God's provision. The miraculous gift of our two children through the adoption, our church home in both Arizona and Colorado, the Lord's gift of consistent employment both during the school year and during the summer, the blessing of doctors and medical professionals who have helped Margaret, the love of friends and family to help us endure, timely teachings and encouragements, and on and on it goes. The list is significant and impacting. God does care for his children. If sickness or disability is a part of your family, he will take care of you. He will provide for you.

I would like to conclude this section with blessing number four: *Encouraging Others*. As I shared in the previous chapter, if you are a Christian, no matter how severe your medical circumstances may be, you are an indispensible member of the body of Christ. God's desire for your life is to not only receive from him, but also to demonstrate his love to other people. The Lord wants to use you to bless others. Over the years Margaret and I have come to understand this more clearly: all the Lord has done for us is not just for us. His love and care has been poured out on us so we in turn can bless others. This is how the body of Christ should function: mutual care for one another.

"Eternal Hope"

The most influential scripture that has motivated us to write this book is 2 Corinthians 1:7: "Our hope for you is unshaken, for we know that as you share in our sufferings, you will also share in our comfort." We have lived, and are living, a life rearranged by the impact of chronic disease. You are most likely reading this book because you and your family are dealing with similar sufferings. Here's the good news: just as you have shared in our type of sufferings, we know you can share in our comfort. This is what the Bible says. This is the Christian reality for the disabled, sick, and their families—shared sufferings with shared comfort in the body of Christ.

Hopefully hearing of God's care in our lives is strengthening you. If we ever have a chance to meet, I know hearing of the Lord's love to you in your medical battles will encourage us. This is one of the sweet aspects of being in the body of Christ. We can influence each other for good. We can help each other to hope when our circumstances seem hopeless. We can be ambassadors of comfort to each other because we are united to the great Comforter.

We have been humbled to know, despite our own weaknesses, that God has used us to strengthen others. Often over the years people have come to us and thanked us for our friendship. They have told us they have been encouraged by our example. Knowing all the times I have sinned, there is no doubt in my mind this encouragement can only be attributed to Jesus' love for us. Since Christ is in our lives, we can bear fruit that builds his body. Yes, because the Lord is with us in our chronic illness world, we can actually be a blessing to our fellow Christians. How grateful I am for the miracle of our salvation! How I thank God that he has been with us through every moment of Margaret's illness!

Let me drive this home just a bit more. I know persevering with a serious health problem is not fun. The pressures, pain, and all that comes with it can easily tempt us to think we have nothing to offer anyone. After all, we sick folk require more care than a lot of people. But I would plead with you to embrace a biblical view of your life. The Lord wants to use you to bless others. God will send people your way who need encouragement (probably sooner than later). He will bring someone across your path that needs to hear how Christ has taken care of you. It has happened to us numerous times—and I am certain your opportunities are coming as well.

The most moving example we have seen of God using us to help others was on a very hot summer day in Arizona. After dinner we had decided to go to our local grocery store. With the children strapped in their car seats we headed out, hoping to accomplish the bulk of our weekly food shopping. After a fairly normal grocery store experience (as normal as it could be with an infant and toddler), we checked out, put the groceries in the car, and secured the kids back in their car seats.

As we started to head home, Margaret began to struggle with some stabbing chest pain. As I saw the dark clouds forming in the southern evening sky, I knew why. Once again her illness was showing its bond to changes in barometric pressure. We were almost home when the monsoon storm hit. The barrage of wind, rain, and lightning filled the sky, and Margaret's level of discomfort continued to escalate. To our dismay, it

"Eternal Hope"

was time for a repeat performance of "with the rain comes the pain."

As I parked our white station wagon in its designated covered apartment parking space, I knew we were going to need some help. Margaret would need my assistance climbing the stairs to our second floor apartment. With both kids and a bunch of groceries in the car, this was a job for more than just me.

Thankfully, I spotted one of our neighbors just a few yards away. She was a kind, tall lady in her mid-twenties that we had gotten to know a bit in our few months living in the complex. Through the gusts of wind and the large rain drops I asked her if she could help us for a few minutes. She politely offered to stay with Margaret and the children while I lugged the white plastic bags of groceries into our residence. I remember seeing her, squatting down as if in a catcher's stance, next to Margaret's open passenger side door. Since my food transport duties required multiple trips to and from the car, the ladies had a few minutes to talk.

Their conversation took a direction that we never could have anticipated. After just a few moments, she shared this story: "Margaret, earlier today I drove to an abortion clinic. As I sat in my car, thinking about what I was about to do, you came to mind. Then I thought to myself, if Margaret is sick and can care for two young children, can't I, by myself, care for one child? Thinking about you made me realize I didn't need an abortion. So, I've decided to keep the baby."

God used Margaret's perseverance to influence a watchful neighbor. A child's life was spared. Thank God for his work of grace in Margaret! Yes, because of what Christ has done for us, we can be a blessing to other people!

How about you? As a believer with a chronic health condition (or a caregiver for an ill loved one), do you see how the Lord wants to use you to encourage others? Do you understand how indispensible you are to Christ's body? Maybe you won't be a part of something as dramatic as saving an unborn child's life—but the Lord wants you to be a vessel of blessing. Pray for those you know who are in need. Ask God how you can help them. Then move out in faith and be a messenger of hope. Make a phone call. Drop a card in the mail. Do whatever you can to enrich the life of someone you know.

Now we get to the final part of the last chapter. I am not just talking about our book. I am talking about the ultimate destination of every believer of every age. This is where, you, as a Christian, are headed. It is the place where all our bodily suffering will cease in the splendor of being in the very presence of Christ. Are you ready to focus on your eternal home? I know we can't wait to get there.

Heaven—Our Eternal Home

Ever since I got my driver's license, it has been clear to me I wasn't born with a good sense of direction. Particularly in upstate New York, where there are few visible landmarks on the horizon, getting lost seemed a normal part of my driving experience. There were times when I would miss an exit on the interstate, only to discover the navigational error of my ways several minutes later. Even when visiting locations for the third or

"Eternal Hope"

fourth time, I never could seem to quite remember how to get there. In fact, at times I couldn't even remember what "there" really looked like. I sort of knew where I was going, but when I came upon a crucial fork in the road, I often resorted to the laws of probability. If the odds seemed in my favor to turn right, I did. Yet this mathematically-based guesswork wasn't very dependable. I just couldn't keep straight how to get where I needed to be, and when I did arrive, the place just didn't seem to look quite the way I remembered it.

This is why over the past few years I have built a tight bond with driving-direction websites. Their online, pinpoint, navigational instructions have saved me a lot of grief. The powers of the internet have also provided a picture of my desired location, so I have a visual image of where I am headed. Additionally, the Rocky Mountains have been my friend; they are my daytime compass to west, so if I get turned around I at least have a point of reference. Then, this year, I was really blessed when my dad sent me a GPS for my car. This cool satellite-driven device not only shows me where I need to go, it *tells* me where I need to go. So, between the combined forces of the internet, the mountains, and my GPS, I no longer agonize over finding my desired location. I know these navigational tools will get me to my destination.

Thank God, in our Christian lives, we don't have to depend on technology or geography to navigate to our final destination. By his grace, we can have real hope for the future by having a deep-rooted understanding of where we are going. We can be certain where all these years of pain and suffering are leading us to. You see, every turn, every unpleasant circumstance, every pain-permeated day is all part of our God-designed, personal road map to get us home. Sure, others may not have to traverse as many rough, pot-holed roads as we do. But that shouldn't discourage us. The Lord is mapping out our lives according to his perfect plan. And, ultimately, triumphantly, we will complete our travels arriving at a final destination too glorious to describe in words. Yes, for the Christian, all our pain and suffering will pale on that day; for our home is heaven, and the Lord promises to bring us safely there. Be inspired as you read these thoughts from the heart of C.H. Spurgeon:

> As surely as you are a child of God today, then just as surely your trials will soon come to an end, and you will be rich in every way with great joy and happiness. Wait a little while and your weary head will be adorned with the crown of glory and your now laboring hands will grasp the palm of victory. . .Do not lament your troubles, but rejoice that soon you will be where "there will be no more death or mourning or crying or pain" (Rev. 21:4). . . Never doubt you will fail to enter this place of rest, for if the Lord has called you, nothing "will be able to separate [you] from the love of God" (Rom. 8:39). . .You are secure, for the Voice who called you at first will call you once again—from earth to heaven and from death's dark gloom to immortality's unspeakable splendor. Rest assured that the heart of Him who justified you beats with infinite love toward you. You will soon

be with the glorified where your inheritance awaits you.[42]

What is heaven like? The prophet Ezekiel (Ezekiel 1) and the Apostle John (Revelation 4) provide for us a picture of the splendor of heaven (feel free to pause and read these chapters if you'd like—they are filled with amazing imagery). John MacArthur summaries their descriptions this way:

> It is impossible to ignore the fact that both Ezekiel and John are describing a scene of breathtaking grandeur and dazzling beauty—a glory that far surpasses the limits of human language. John, like Ezekiel, is painting a big picture that portrays heaven as a bright, colorful realm of inexpressible splendor and delight... Language fails when humans try to describe divine glory, so John is using these comparisons to precious jewels to picture the breathtaking beauty of heavenly glory. The jewels he mentions were the most stunning, glorious images he could picture, so he resorts to them to make his point. Remember, though, that he is actually describing a glory that far exceeds that of any jewel dug out of the earth. If the scene is hard for you to visualize, that's fine. John is purposely painting a picture of glory that exceeds our ability to imagine.[43]

Heaven is so glorious, it is beyond our human ability to describe. Going there is the destiny of every believer of all ages. Old Testament believers are there.

Always Sick, Always Loved

New Testament believers are there. But most importantly, God the Father is there. Jesus, our loving Lord and Savior is there. Yes, one day, you and I will have the most wonderful reunion of our lives. We will see departed Christian loved ones. We will meet believers from every era of world history. What a day that will be! Let's hear again from John MacArthur:

> In reality, everything that is truly precious to us as Christians is in heaven. . . The *Father* is there (Matthew 6:9). . . *Jesus* himself is at the Father's right hand. . . So our Savior is also in heaven, where he intercedes on our behalf (Hebrews 7:25). . .Many *brothers and sisters in Christ* are there too (Hebrews 12:22-24). . . Our departed loved ones in the faith are there with Christ and with the Father. Every Old and New Testament believer who has died is now in heaven. . . Our *names* are recorded there (Luke 10:20). . . And by saying that our names are written in heaven, Christ assures us that we have a title deed to property there. This is *our inheritance* (1 Peter 1:4).[44]

As Christians, we are on a journey that will ultimately take us home. Home is heaven. Our getting there is guaranteed by our Savior. Heaven is a real place we should think about and long for. As the scriptures say, "If you then have been raised with Christ, seek the things that are above, where Christ is, seated at the right hand of God" (Colossians 3:1).

Yes, Margaret's current medical prognosis isn't a good one. Her death very well could be sooner than

"Eternal Hope"

later. But don't feel sorry for us. Every moment of her illness, from the original onset of her symptoms to where she physically is today, has been part of the Lord's plan. This we are sure of. God designed a road map for our lives that has included the bumpy road of chronic disease. Yet his planned journey for us has always had a divine purpose. Its goal has been to teach us about his love. These rough streets have shown us our weakness, and his supernatural strength. We have been able to know our Savior more. The older we get, the more we want to see Jesus face to face. We want to run to him, embrace him, and thank him for all he has done for us. You see, heaven means going home. It means coming into the very presence of the One you have grown to love more than anything in the world.

So, nowadays Margaret and I talk often about heaven. We discuss what it will be like, and how exciting it will be for her to see Jesus and to reunite with her mom and dad. Recently she said to me, "You know, I wonder if I am going to die pretty soon." When I asked her why she felt this way, she explained, "I feel like someone who has been on a long journey. And now, as the trip nears its end, you feel homesick; you know, you just look forward to going home."

Yes, she longs to go home; not in a negative, "I am sick of my illness and want to get out of here" escapist kind of way. She wants to embrace her Savior. She looks forward to reuniting with her deceased loved ones. And, as much as I want to spend many more years with her, I know that one day, maybe sooner than I'd like, the Lord will fulfill the longing of her heart and take her home.

Here is an incredible paradox of Christianity: the day we die, is the greatest day of our lives. Why? When our bodies expire our souls are immediately in Christ's presence. A believer's death is his ticket to heaven. This is why we can say with the Apostle Paul, "We would rather be away from the body and at home with the Lord" (2 Corinthians 5:8), and "For to me to live is Christ, and to die is gain. . . My desire is to depart and be with Christ, for that is far better" (Philippians 1:21,23).

So when the day of Margaret's death comes, she will experience the most spectacular event of her life—being in heaven, seeing her Savior, and worshipping and rejoicing with all the saints of all ages. She will enter into the visible reality of eternal life with Christ.

I have already mentioned some of the glorious attributes of heaven: its unimaginable beauty, and the preciousness of who will be there. Want to hear a few more highlights? First, "He will wipe away every tear from their eyes, and death shall be no more, neither shall there be mourning, nor crying, nor pain anymore, for the former things have passed away" (Revelation 21:4). Incredibly, no more crying, no more tears, no more pain, no more death. All types of suffering will never again afflict us. Sin, and all its nasty effects will be permanently removed from us. Praise God for the salvation we have in Christ, and our home in heaven!

Secondly, as mysterious as it seems, in heaven the Lord will reward us for our perseverance. There will be a special divine payday based on how we lived our lives. This payday isn't to earn our salvation. Faith in Christ's atoning work is the only means for forgiveness of sins and eternal life. But the Bible is clear that crowns will be given. Our toil and faithfulness to the

"Eternal Hope"

Lord will be evaluated. I don't understand how all this works (particularly since God gives us the strength to serve him), but the giving of rewards is a clear teaching of scripture. James 1:12 states, "Blessed is the man who remains steadfast under trial, for when he has stood the test he will receive the crown of life." Also, 2 Corinthians 5:9-10 states, "So whether we are at home or away, we make it our aim to please him. For we must all appear before the judgment seat of Christ, so that each one may receive what is due for what he has done in the body, whether good or evil."

Yes, once we leave this life, God says everyone will "receive what is due." We will hear God's evaluation of what we did with the years he gave us. Hear these encouraging words from Wayne Grudem:

> In our own lives a heartfelt seeking of future heavenly reward would motivate us to work wholeheartedly for the Lord at whatever task he calls us to do, whether great or small, paid or unpaid. It would also make us long for his approval rather than for wealth or success. It would motivate us to work at building up the church on the one foundation, Jesus Christ (1 Corinthians 3:10-15).[45]

As Margaret's primary caregiver, this summarizes my greatest motivation in caring for her. One day, in the presence of God, I long to hear his "thank you." As I look into his eyes, I desire to hear him say he was pleased with how I cared for Margaret and my family. My sins and failures forgiven, when I enter into eternity I want to know his pleasure. So, too, if you have given

Always Sick, Always Loved

your life to care for a chronically ill family member, understand the Lord is well aware of your labor. He knows all the sacrifices you have made. And one day it will be worth it all—when you see his face, and hear his gratitude for all you have done.

You see, God is keeping track. He knows all we go through and experience in the land of chronic illness. Through Christ we are saved from the wrath and eternal judgment for our sins. By his love, we will be rewarded for our life of perseverance. Whether you are a patient or a caregiver, remember—what we see now is only a very small part of our eternal existence. One day, it will be worth it all, when we are in God's dwelling place, with him for all of eternity.

Finally, as my last highlight of heaven, understand that one day, the Day, when Jesus returns, we will be resurrected. The souls of those in heaven will be permanently reunited with their earthly bodies. But their bodies will be completely transformed—resurrected and made new, just like Christ's resurrected body. Yes, the same bodies that afflict us and limit us now will be supernaturally changed. Believers who have already died will resurrect first, instantly followed by the living Christians. Our bodily resurrection is certain. This truth is an undeniable teaching of scripture. One day Jesus is coming back. And when he does, we will be with him. Rejoice in this eternal reality, expressed in 1 Thessalonians 4:15-18:

> For this we declare to you by a word from the Lord, that we who are alive, who are left until the coming of the Lord, will not precede those who have fallen asleep. For the Lord himself will

"Eternal Hope"

descend from heaven with a cry of command, with the voice of an archangel, and with the sound of the trumpet of God. And the dead in Christ will rise first. Then we who are alive, who are left, will be caught up together with them in the clouds to meet the Lord in the air, and so we will always be with the Lord. Therefore encourage one another with these words.

What a hope. What a great salvation. What a Savior! So now, I once again make my plea. Are you a Christian, who due to your medical challenges, have allowed your heart to grow cold and bitter toward the Lord? I have been there. Anger, despair and hopelessness can be a real cancer to your soul. As you have read of Christ's love, and the glorious hope we have in him, do you desire to renew your relationship with Jesus? Come freshly to him. Pour your heart out to him. Openly share all your hurts, confusion and struggles. He will not turn you away. He will welcome you with open arms. Maybe you have been angry with him for years. His love extends way beyond any and all of your sins. His desire is to touch your heart with his love. The Lord has done it for us, and I know he wants to do it for you. He longs to be intimately involved in your life. He wants to give you supernatural comfort and encouragement in all you are going through. So, please, make the Lord your refuge in your medical battle. He will take care of all your needs.

If you are not a Christian, do you sense your need of Jesus? Has he been tugging at your heart, inviting you to put your total trust in him for your salvation? He invites you to begin a relationship with him today.

Always Sick, Always Loved

Please read again the message of the gospel in chapter two. Respond to his loving call, pointing you to Christ. Believe on the Lord Jesus, so that you might be saved.

I conclude our book with what I pray has been a steady and undeniable theme: Jesus Christ, God in the flesh, is our only hope for salvation. He also is our only hope in this life; the One who enables us to endure chronic disease and disability. His gospel tells us of his eternal love for us. His word provides soul-stabilizing truth to help us keep the right perspective. As our loving high priest, he understands everything about our struggles. He delights in spending time with us each day. He lovingly teaches us contentment. He gives us practical wisdom. He provides eternal hope for our future. Praise God, on the day of our death, we will enter into his dwelling place, heaven, for all of eternity. All our pain, disease, and disability will cease in a sea of endless worship in the very presence of Jesus Christ. Thank you Lord, for your salvation! Thank you for your endless care! Come quickly Lord Jesus. We long to see you face to face. Amen.

Discussion Questions

1) Please read the 23rd Psalm. What truths in this Psalm encourage you the most?
2) As you reflect on your experience with health problems, where have you seen the Lord's love and care? Which of these are you most thankful for and why?
3) Do you know you are going to heaven when you die? What biblical truths assure you of this? What do you most look forward to

"Eternal Hope"

experiencing in heaven? (If you are not sure you are going to heaven when you die, please reread chapter two).

Thank you for taking the time to read our book. We'd appreciate hearing your feedback. Feel free to email us at *mmrobble25@gmail.com*.

Endnotes

1. D.A. Carson, *How Long O Lord?* (Grand Rapids, Michigan: Baker Books, 1990), 16.

2. ICare Health Monitoring, Inc. Website, May 2007.

3. Michael Agnes, Editor in Chief, *Webster's New World Dictionary* (Cleveland, Ohio: Wiley Publishing, 2003), 118.

4. John B. Leuzarder, *The Gospel for Children* (Wapwallopen, Pennsylvania: Shepherd Press, 2002), 13.

5. Jerry Bridges, *The Gospel for Real Life* (Colorado Springs, Colorado: NavPress, 2002), 18.

6. Jerry Bridges, *The Discipline of Grace*, (Colorado Springs, Colorado: NavPress, 1994), 45.

7. John Piper, *Fifty Reasons Why Jesus Came to Die*, (Wheaton, Illinois: Crossway Books, 2006), 30.

8. John MacArthur, *The MacArthur Study Bible,* (Wheaton, Illinois: Crossway Books, 2010), 1575.

9. Carson, *How Long O Lord*, 47.

10. C.J. Mahaney, *The Cross Centered Life*, (Sistera, Oregon: Multnomah Publishers, 2002), 84.

11. *The American Heritage Dictionary*, (New York, New York: Bantam Dell, 2007), 91.

12. Wayne Grudem, *Bible Doctrine*, (Grand Rapids, Michigan: Zondervan, 1999), 20.

13. J.I. Packer, *Concise Theology*, (Wheaton, Illinois: Tyndale House, 1993), 33.

14. Jerry Bridges, *Trusting God*, (Colorado Springs, Colorado: NavPress, 1988), 46.

15. Timothy Keller, *Walking with God through Pain and Suffering,* (New York, New York: Dutton, 2013), 285.

16. Jerry Bridges, Bob Bevington, *Bookends of the Christian Life,* (Wheaton, Illinois: Crossway Books, 2009), 82.

17. Joni Eareckson Tada, *When God Weeps*, (Grand Rapids, Michigan: Zondervan Publishing House, 1997), 56.

18. John R. W. Stott, *The Cross of Christ,* (Downers Grove, Illinois: InterVarsity Press, 1986), 216.

19. Mahaney, *The Cross Centered Life*, 61-62.

20. Great-quotes.com, November, 2014

21. Linda Dillow, *Calm My Anxious Heart*, (Colorado Springs, Colorado: NavPress, 1998), 116.

22. J.A. Motyer, *The Message of Philippians,* (Downers Grove, Illinois: Inter-Varsity Press, 1984), 207-208.

23. Joni Eareckson Tada, *Diamonds in the Dust*, (Grand Rapids, Michigan: Zondervan, 1993), July 7 Devotional.

24. MacArthur, *The MacArthur Study Bible,* 781.

25. David Powlison, *The Journal of Biblical Counseling,* Volume 18, Number 3, Spring 2000.

26. John Piper, *A Godward Life,* (Sisters, Oregon: Multnomah Publishers, Inc., 1997), 24.

Endnotes

27. James G. Reimann, *Look Unto Me*, (Grand Rapids, Michigan: Zondervan, 2008), Day 153.

28. Motyer, *The Message of Philippians*, 220.

29. Tara Parker-Pope, NY Times.com, June, 2009.

30. *The Amplified Bible*, (Grand Rapids, Michigan: Zondervan, 1987), 1827.

31. *The American Heritage Dictionary*, 528.

32. Searchquotes.com, November 2014

33. Brett Hoover, quoted in Hepstrack.com, June, 2013.

34. *The Amplified Bible*, 1733.

35. Packer, *Concise Theology*, 202.

36. Packer, *Concise Theology*, 98.

37. Margaret Clarkson, *Grace Grows Best in Winter*, (Grand Rapids, Michigan: Zondervan, 1972), 9-10.

38. Paul E. Miller, *A Praying Life*, (Colorado Springs, Colorado: Navpress, 2009), 23-24.

39. Kathleen Romito MD, Adam Husney MD, Anne C. Poinier MD, Healthwise Staff, Kaiser Permanente, kp.org, December, 2010.

40. W. Phillip Keller, *A Shepherd Looks at Psalm 23*, (Grand Rapids, Michigan: Zondervan, 1970), 70.

41. Keller, *A Shepherd Looks at Psalm 23*, 101,103.

42. James G. Reimann, *Look Unto Me*, Day 149.

43. John MacArthur, *The Glory of Heaven*, (Wheaton, Illinois: Crossway, 2013), 98.

44. MacArthur, *The Glory of Heaven*, 66-67.

45. Grudem, *Bible Doctrine*, 457.

CPSIA information can be obtained at www.ICGtesting.com
Printed in the USA
BVOW05s0039040315

390170BV00001B/18/P